WOMEN WHO KILL VICIOUSLY

Edited by Mike James

D0681081

PAN BOOKS

First published 1999 by True Crime Library

This edition published 2003 by Pan Books
an imprint of Pan Macmillan Ltd
Pan Macmillan, 20 New Wharf Road, London N1 99R
Basingstoke and Oxford
Associated companies throughout the world
www.panmacmillan.com

ISBN 0 330 42108 5

3 5 7 9 8 6 4 2

A CIP catalogue record for this book is available from
the British Library.

Printed and bound in Great Britain by
Mackays of Chatham plc, Chatham, Kent

With thanks to
Roy Minton.
Essential to every
one of our publications

The complete
TRUE CRIME LIBRARY

A NEW CENTURY OF SEX KILLERS
FATAL ATTRACTION
A DATE WITH THE HANGMAN
MURDER WITH VENOM
BRITAIN'S GODFATHER
ON DEATH ROW
WOMEN ON DEATH ROW
BEDSIDE BOOK OF MURDER
LOVE YOU TO DEATH
STRANGE TALES FROM STRANGEWAYS
DIARY OF A HANGMAN
FROM WALL STREET TO NEWGATE
CAMINADA THE CRIMEBUSTER
FROM THE X-FILES OF MURDER
FAR FROM THE LAND
THE CORPSE GARDEN
THE BOOTLEGGERS
CLASSIC MURDERS OF THE NORTH EAST
WOMEN WHO KILL VICIOUSLY
MURDER ONE
CLASSIC MURDERS OF THE NORTH WEST

CONTENTS

Preface   1

1. Honeymoon of Horror   3
   Don Lasseter

2. Human Sacrifice   21
   Bill Kelly

3. Road Rage   33
   Brian Marriner

4. Death Row Interview With Rhonda Belle Martin   55
   Allen Rankin

5. The Trouble With Judy   69
   Sam Roen and A.W. Moss

6. Castrated With Scissors   83
   Ed Browning

7. Breaking Point   93
   Brian Marriner

8. Sexual Persuasion   107
   Martin Lomax

9. A High Degree of Callousness   117
   Don Lasseter

10. The Black Widow   131
    Brian Marriner

11. Mother Love   145
    David Drew

12. The Badger Game   161
William Kendal

13. The Foxes in the Wood Murder   175
Brian Marriner

14. Psycho Woman   187
Bill Kelly

15. Death of a Private Eye   195
Brian Marriner

16. Sex, Lies and Murder   205
Charles Sasser

17. Devil Bitch From Hell   215
Charles Sasser

18. Recipe For Murder   223
Richard Devon

PREFACE

As women who kill are such a rare breed, this paperback is a great find for both the connoisseur and the uninitiated. Many of the murder stories are as diverse and compelling as the women themselves. The editor gently weaves common threads between relevant cases without dampening the effect of letting the crimes speak for themselves.

There are similarities in some of the crimes, and there are huge differences. Some of the women were abused, others were driven by jealousy or greed, and many were obviously clinically ill while strewing their paths with the dead bodies of loved ones. There are others who were perfectly sane and strong, who used men for their own material gain, and killed them when they were no longer of any use to them.

The book opens with the horrific Omaima Nelson story which leaves no doubt as to how vicious a woman can be. However, there is a strong argument for Omaima's defence because she came from a Cairo slum; was circumcised without anaesthetic at the age of six, raped when she was 10 years old, and again when she was 19, and made an outcast within her own culture.

She was, however, a survivor who married an American to escape her past and emigrated to the land of plenty. After divorcing her first husband, she found work as a nanny and a model, and married again — a man much older than herself, who she thought would be kind to her. But she ended up cutting him into little pieces, barbecuing and eating his ribs. Was this the handiwork of an abused outcast, or retaliation from an evil woman?

After being offered the ribs of Bill Nelson as a starter, the following stories are somehow more palatable, although no less gruesome. Yet the book is not just a catalogue of bloody gore, there is a fascinating Death Row interview with Rhonda Belle Martin who would love somebody to tell her just why she murdered members of her family... again and again and again.

Included are murder cases from America, England, and Australia and it is very interesting to compare the attitudes of the women in each continent. The English murderess is cool and caluculating, whereas the American leans towards a confused, emotional approach.

One thing the stories do reveal is that the idea of women as a frail and gentle breed is as spurious as the concept of men being strong and masterful.

1

HONEYMOON OF HORROR

Don Lasseter

"I barbecued his ribs, just like in a restaurant"

STILL DROWSY after sleeping late on Sunday morning, December 1st, 1991, John Popovich saw the red Corvette pull up in front of his house for the second time.

Earlier that morning, at about 9.15, he had been awakened by a loud knock on his front door. Irritated by the intrusion, Popovich had pulled aside his bedroom window blind, glanced out at the sporty red car, grunted drowsily, and pulled the covers back over his head. He didn't know anyone who drove a Corvette with Texas licence plates. The caller must be for his room-mate, he thought, and he curled up and went back to sleep.

Now, a little after noon, Popovich stood at his front door and watched as the Corvette screeched to a halt at the kerb. An exotic young woman dressed in tight-fitting trousers, black gloves; a loose white blouse, and dark glasses, scrambled from the driver's seat and hurried towards him. Popovich knew her, but he had never seen her drive a red Corvette. She was trembling, crying, and "all shook up."

"I've been raped," she sobbed, and proceeded to tell

Popovich the most grisly, horrifying sequence of events he had ever heard.

Omaima Nelson had previously visited John Popovich several times at his home in Costa Mesa, California. he new her as "Ishta." During the hot summer months she had been a guest at a few of his barbecues. Popovich had also occasionally noticed the curvaceous 23-year-old woman enjoying the music and dancing at a local bar. That was before her recent marriage.

"My husband just raped me and cut me," Omaima wept. "Can you help me?" She accepted Popovich's offer of a cigarette, and removed a black glove, along with her dark glasses. Popovich saw that the bare hand was marked with cuts and scrapes, some covered with plastic bandages. Whimpering, Omaima described how her husband had bound her to the bed and forced her to have repeated "kinky" sex.

Popovich would later relate for the police the beginning of Omaima's story: "She said her husband tied her up ... that he had been drinking and I guess taking drugs. He was having sex, and forcing her to have oral sex. There was physical abuse ... He was cutting her."

Her wounds, Omaima told Popovich, might require some first aid. She would show him.

While Popovich watched in astonishment, Omaima lifted her blouse, pulled her right breast from the top of her bra, and revealed two parallel scratches, over two inches long, oozing small amounts of blood. Then, without any sign of inhibition, Omaima began to unbutton her tight black trousers to show him even more.

"She pulled her pants down," Popovich would subsequently recall, "but I could already see the cut on her thigh. It was kind of visible through the vents on the side of her pants."

Standing before him in her underwear, Omaima Nelson displayed her various wounds. Her wrists, Popovich thought, "had signs of being tied up." The wounds even extended to a toe that bled when she removed the gauze bandage.

Despite her injuries, Omaima wasn't bad to look at. With her olive complexion, shoulder-length brown hair, and voluptuous 5-foot-1 figure, she frequently caught the attention of men's wandering eyes. Her high cheekbones, wide mouth and sinuously full lips, and smouldering brown eyes gave her an exotic sex appeal.

Born in Egypt in 1968, Omaima brought to mind the mysteries of Nefertiti or the eroticism of veiled dancers. She had recently been employed as a model.

John Popovich knew some of her background, but not all of it.

As a young child, Omaima Aref had lived in a squatter's section of Cairo known as the "city of the dead," so named because of its proximity to cemeteries. She was one of eight children, and she had been sexually abused and painfully circumcised, without the use of anaesthesia, when she was six years old.

Omaima was raped for the first time at the age of 10 and again at 19. In Moslem culture, she later confided, her loss of virginity would create serious problems if she married. A future husband's discovery of her violated purity could result in harsh punishment for her and dishonour for her whole family. She feared that it might lead to her being killed.

So when at 19, Omaima met a young American, she married him and moved to the United States in 1986, to escape her hopeless future in her native land.

Omaima's marriage soon floundered, and she struggled with a series of unsatisfactory relationships before being divorced in 1990. She found work in Southern California as a nanny and as a department store model. In the autumn of 1991, in the Costa Mesa tavern she frequented to dance and listen to music, she met William Nelson, a brawny six-footer who, at 56, was 33 years her senior.

"It was really nice," Omaima told her friends. "He was a gentleman." Bill would open the door for her and take her out to dinner. "I was in love. I was looking for someone who was kind and nice and wouldn't beat up on me and would give me love . . . love I never found before."

Nice as he was William Nelson was also an ex-convict. Before he met Omaima, he had served four years in prison for drug trafficking and tax-evasion. Upon his release, he had resettled in Costa Mesa.

Nelson took the beautiful young Egyptian to Phoenix, Arizona, and married her on the first day of November 1991. They spent the first part of their honeymoon driving cross-country, through Arkansas and Texas, where Bill acquired the sporty red Corvette and the last week they spent at home. Now, after four short weeks of marriage, something was terribly wrong.

The words that spilled from Omaima Nelson brought John Popovich back to reality, and nearly sent him into shock.

The horrifying litany, as she put her clothes on, was interrupted by another knock at the door. Popovich whispered to Omaima to remain calm and not to worry. He cautiously opened the door just a crack, peered out, and was relieved to see only a friendly woman neighbour. Before letting her in, he cautioned Omaima.

"It will be better not to tell the neighbour what has happened," Popovich whispered. "She goes to church and she's a real peaceful person. I don't want to scare her. Let's just say that you got in a brawl with your old man or some girl." Omaima understood, and when the neighbour entered, she explained that the cuts on her hands were a result of a domestic dispute. The kindly visitor offered to clean, treat, and bandage the wounds.

Mulling over Omaima's request for help, Popovich finally decided what he must do. After telling her that he would assist her, he made an excuse to go to a shop first. The visiting neighbour would give him a lift, Omaima agreed to wait in the house.

Popovich left with his neighbour. From the first public telephone he saw, the distressed young man telephoned the Costa Mesa police.

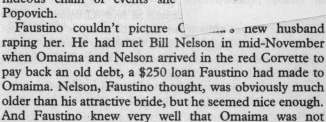

The sanctuary Omaima so
her only plea for help that
hadn't responded to her earlie
the Corvette a few miles away
friend, George Faustino, with
various times during the five y
At 10.30 a.m., crying hysterically
hideous chain of events she
Popovich.

Faustino couldn't picture O_____ new husband
raping her. He had met Bill Nelson in mid-November
when Omaima and Nelson arrived in the red Corvette to
pay back an old debt, a $250 loan Faustino had made to
Omaima. Nelson, Faustino thought, was obviously much
older than his attractive bride, but he seemed nice enough.
And Faustino knew very well that Omaima was not
ordinarily resistant to sex.

Just as she would with John Popovich, Omaima stripped
to her underwear and bared her breast to show the wounds
to her ex-lover while she begged him to help her. Faustino
still felt friendly towards her, but he didn't want to be
involved. It would be better if she left, he told her. In tears,
she returned to Popovich's house, and shocked him with
her story.

Popovich had no choice but to notify the police.

At 2.05 p.m. Officer Danny Hogue arrived at Popovich's
house to question Omaima Nelson. A former member of
the homicide squad, Hogue was an experienced inter-
viewer. Omaima, although startled at finding the police
suddenly involved, answered his questions calmly. She
told Hogue that her husband, Bill Nelson, was away on a
business trip in Florida. She didn't know exactly where he
was staying in Florida or when he would return.

Because of the nature of the report by Popovich, Officer
Hogue asked Omaima's permission to search the Corvette.
She did not object, and oddly volunteered that he would
find no "coke" even though, she said, she had "done"
some approximately 20 minutes earlier. A subsequent

d no trace of cocaine.

istered to William Nelson was not locked.
ma asked what was going on, and complained
eone was "trying to set her up," the officer looked
and found a plastic rubbish bag. He had to suppress
urge to throw-up when he saw what it contained:
bloody meat and internal organs. He couldn't tell if they
were animal or human.

While another officer remained with Omaima and the
Corvette, Hogue drove the short distance to the address
listed on the car registration for William Nelson. At the
upstairs apartment, there was no answer to his knock, so
he forced his way in. He noted that the inside front
doorknob was bloodstained. Full cardboard boxes near the
entrance and tied plastic rubbish bags in other rooms
suggested that someone had packed to move out. In the
bedroom Hogue saw an open clothes hamper at the foot of
the bed that contained a blood-soaked sheet that was still
wet. A large butcher's knife lay in the kitchen sink.

As a veteran of combat in Vietnam and of innumerable
homicide scenes, Hogue was not rattled by the sight of
blood. He secured the premises and radioed headquarters.

Detective Bob Phillips was enjoying his leisurely Sunday
afternoon by running an antique miniature train, part of
his extensive collection of rare toys. A 13-year veteran of
the police department, he had worked a four-year stint in
narcotics until his recent transfer to homicide. He was
anticipating his first assignment as lead investigator, and
when he answered the phone at 3 p.m., he had it. Phillip's
Thanksgiving weekend was over, and he was on his way to
pick up another detective.

Frank Rudisill's phone rang, interrupting a backyard
barbecue, and he learned that his friend and partner, Bob
Phillips, would pick him up. Rudisill was excited, because
he, too, had transferred from the narcotics squad, and this
would be his first investigation with the new team. So far,
though, it was just a "possible" homicide.

During their drive to the scene Phillips, with remarkable

foresight, remarked to Rudisill, "I've got a feeling this is going to be a house of horrors."

A third member of the team, Lynda Giesler, was brought out of a lazy Sunday nap by her ringing phone. Lynda would lend valuable experience to the job at hand, having become one of the first female detectives in the state, 30 years earlier.

After a short stop at the Popovich home, Detectives Phillips and Giesler obtained Omaima Nelson's agreement to be interviewed at the police station.

In a well-lit room, seated in a comfortable upholstered chair, Omaima faced Giesler and Phillips across a circular oak table. Haltingly, in a soft, trembling voice, she began a rambling story that was virtually impossible to follow.

She repeated that her husband was out of town. With tears streaming down her face again, she said that Nelson had raped her on Thanksgiving Day. She made allusions to strange dreams in which she wondered, "Where's Bill?" and thought, "I don't have Bill's phone number." She vaguely hinted that Nelson had also raped two other girls not long after he had been released from prison, the previous March. The girls were missing, she thought, and their passports were in Bill's possession.

Answering questions between sobs, Omaima said that Nelson had forced her to pose for "thousands" of pornographic photographs.

Because she was again wearing the black gloves, Detective Phillips asked Omaima to remove them. She explained that she had sustained the obvious injuries during a fight with an unknown woman in a bar in nearby Santa Ana. She voluntarily stood up and began to disrobe to show the investigators her other wounds. Detective Giesler listed them, while Phillips gallantly turned his back. Giesler thought it was pecular that a woman claimed to have been brutally raped was so immodest.

Denying any knowledge of the bags in the Corvette, Omaima said that she had given a man a lift to the launderette. Maybe he had left the bags in the car.

Adding more details to the events of Thanksgiving Day, Omaima said that before her husband raped her, they had spent the day with his friends in Riverside. Then a little later in the interview she changed her mind, saying that they had dined at home.

Something wasn't adding up for Phillips. He thought that perhaps the missing ex-convict Bill Nelson had set up a big scam to disappear. The detective made a mental note to pursue that angle if Nelson wasn't found soon. Meanwhile Phillips needed to fill out the paperwork for a warrant to search the apartment, so he released Omaima to be taken to a hospital, where she was given a routine rape examination.

The subsequent report stated that no semen was found in Omaima's body. Her various wounds, a doctor concluded, were sufficiently old for scabbing and preliminary infection to have started.

Detective Phillips asked John Popovich what the Egyptian woman had told him. Still shaken, the witness described how Omaima had arrived at his house, cried about being raped, and stripped to show him her injuries. "Then she asked me if she could trust me with her life." When Popovich asked what she meant, Omaima had given him a stunning reply.

"She told me that she had killed her husband," Popovich divulged. "I asked her how, what happened? She said she was tied up on the bed while he was raping her and cutting her, but she broke loose with her right hand and reached over and grabbed the lamp and smacked her husband over the head with it."

According to Popovich, Omaima said that when Nelson fell unconscious, she grabbed "the tool" he had used to cut her and stabbed him. She had demonstrated it to Popovich with a wild slashing motion, which he re-enacted for the investigator.

Popovich still felt stunned and sickened as he revealed the next part of Omaima's story. "She said that she'd chopped him up in pieces and cut off his head and she wanted me to dispose of it. She said that she had washed the blood off the body parts, wrapped them in newspaper, and put them in plastic bags and left them in the apartment. She wanted me to go over there and do some cleaning."

Omaima had offered Popovich $75,000 and two motorcycles, he disclosed, if he would agree to help clean up the apartment and dispose of her husband's remains.

"She told me she took the head, hands, arms and legs, and other pieces to the bathroom to clean them up and wash off the blood in the bath," Popovich continued. "She washed the parts so they would be drained of blood so they wouldn't drip anywhere." He had agreed to help her, Popovich told Phillips, just to stall for time until he could call the police.

"She told me that when I disposed of the head, I should make sure I crushed it, with the dentures, so there wouldn't be any trace of who it was," Popovich concluded.

Detectives Giesler and Jack Archer later talked to George Faustino, the ex-boy friend who had rejected Omaima's request for help.

"Yeah," he reluctantly told them, making it clear that he didn't like cops, "she told me she killed her husband. She said she was tied, beaten, and raped, and she hit him over the head with a lamp. He was in pieces."

Faustino had seen some cuts on Omaima, but wasn't sure he believed her story. He just wanted her out of there. When she left, he walked to the Corvette with her. He saw some credit cards, in Bill Nelson's name, on the passenger seat of the car.

Back at police headquarters, Omaima denied that she had killed her husband. Instead she claimed, she had received a telephone call. Someone had yelled into the phone, "Well, bitch, you got what you wanted! Look in the trash bag. Why don't you check in the kitchen? You want some hamburger?" She had looked, Omaima said, had seen the grisly remains, and had rushed over to

Popovich's house for help. She thought maybe the bloody mess was someone her husband had killed.

"He's chopped up women before," Omaima claimed. Then she reverted to more accounts of sexual abuse, whimpering that Nelson had made her watch porno-graphic videotapes, and that she had been a "beautiful model" before Nelson "cut her everywhere and made her ugly." She kept asking if she was going to the "gas chair."

"Do you live with your husband at the apartment?" Detective Phillips asked.

"I haven't been there for nearly two weeks," Omaima replied, explaining that Nelson had been in and out of town and he didn't want her to occupy the apartment while he was away. But "a number of people," had keys to the flat.

Phillips used an old investigative gambit. "How do you explain the fact that someone saw you there very recently?"

"It must have been the chick who looks kind of like me. She lives in the complex," Omaima replied. Finally, saying that she wondered if the body parts had been the remains of her husband, Omaima said she wanted to talk to a psychiatrist. The detectives concluded the interview at 10 o'clock that night.

The following afternoon, Detectives Phillips, Giesler and Archer, armed with a search warrant, entered the apartment of Bill Nelson.

The homicide team "rookie," Frank Rudisill, had the task of digging through the huge rubbish bin outside, which was packed to the rim.

"You want to be a homicide detective, don't you?" Phillips asked, grinning. "Well, this is an important part of the job."

Inside, within minutes, the investigators began making grisly discoveries. They opened one of the plastic bags and found human legs severed at the knee. Various other body parts were wrapped in newspaper and stuffed into another plastic bag. One contained human male genitals. From a cardboard box, Giesler removed a newspaper-wrapped bundle, and began to peel away the layers of paper. She recoiled in horror at the sight of a pair of severed hands, with the left ring finger hacked off. It would later be revealed that the hands had been cooked in oil, apparently to destroy the fingerprints.

A forensic scientist accompanying the detectives was curious about the neatly made bed, wondering where the bloodstained sheets had come from. He lifted the heavy mattress, turned it over, and was appalled to find that the entire underside was drenched in blood. Obviously the body had been dismembered on the bed, then someone had removed a sheet wet with blood, turned over the fluid soaked mattress, and carefully made up the bed.

Several boots were standing at strange locations around the room. The technician found when he moved them that each had been placed to cover a bloodstain.

Meanwhile, Rudisill dug through the rubbish in the bin and found a pile of still-frozen, unused boxes of peas, corn, frozen dinners, and other food, obviously removed from a freezer. He raced up the stairs to tell his colleagues that something big was in the freezer.

Slowly, in awful anticipation, the detectives swung open the freezer door. An innocuous blue plastic tray, filled with foil-wrapped packages, was all they saw. Detective Archer lifted out the largest package and began to unwrap it. He cringed in horror when he peeled back the last layer.

Shrunken, sightless eyes gazed at him from a grinning skull. Some of the skin had been boiled away, and the jaws were blackened and charred from being partially cooked. The head had been scalped. The hairy flap of skin that had been sliced off the skull was found in another package.

Detective Giesler found a portable ice chest, and when she lifted the top she was met by the stench of blood. Clothing and rags stuffed into the chest had apparently been used to mop up the gore.

The search also turned up the passports of two young women. In the bedroom was a portfolio of colour photographs of a smiling Omaima Nelson. In some she wore nothing but white panties and a bra; in others, she was completely nude. Detective Archer found a steam iron, bent and bloodstained, which he carefully put in an evidence bag.

In a most unusual departure from normal procedure, the pathologist, Dr. Ronald Katsuyama, was brought to the crime scene to begin an autopsy examination. He would later have the body parts taken to his lab, where he would spread the remains on a stainless steel table in a macabre reassembly for identification. The body parts proved to be all that was left of the missing William Nelson.

Omaima Nelson was arrested at 5.55 p.m., on suspicion of murder.

Detective Phillips and his team then began the long process of interviewing prospective witnesses. The resident of a neighbouring apartment said that he had last seen Bill Nelson in front of the building at a little after noon on Thanksgiving Day. He had seen Omaima on Sunday, December 1st, while he was washing his car. She had arrived in the Corvette, parked near the rubbish bin, and disappeared into the apartment. Moments later, she reappeared carrying a rectangular rubbish bag which she started to throw into the bin, but she apparently changed her mind.

Another neighbour had overheard "chopping noises," and was irritated by Nelson's waste disposal running most of the night. The information was no surprise to the detectives, since they had dismantled the plumbing and found traces of human flesh. Remarkably, there had been no odour in the apartment, and the first stench came from the open drain tap below the sink.

After the sensational case hit the newspapers, one more acquaintance of Omaima Nelson came forward. Orville Whittaker, who had known her since 1989, reported that she had been with him in his bedroom in November 1990. He said, "Well, she wanted to have sex with me, and so we went upstairs to the bedroom, and she says, 'Let me tie your hands. Don't worry I'm not going to hurt you or anything.' " Whittaker added that Omaima used two of his neckties to bind his wrists to the bedpost.

"After she got my hands tied, she pulled a gun out and she put it to my face and says she wanted for me to give her money. I thought she was kidding. I really did. You know, I was laughing." He told her to put the gun away, Whittaker said, "because, you know, something could happen." But Omaima refused, and demanded money.

"I finally got one hand free from the left hand side," Whittaker continued, "and then I got up and got my other hand free, and I pushed her back against the dresser. I took the gun away, and told her to get the heck out. She left and I kept her gun."

"What were you both wearing?"

"She was in her panties and I was wearing shorts."

Asked about their prior relationship, Whittaker said that Omaima had lived with him for three or four months. Shortly after she left him, he was furious because he received a department store bill for $1,600. When he checked he found that his credit card for that particular store was missing.

Detective Phillips tracked down the women whose passports were found in Bill Nelson's apartment. Contrary to Omaima's suggestion that both were missing, they were alive and well. They explained that their passports had been stolen in New York in May 1990. They didn't know, nor had they ever heard of, Bill or Omaima Nelson. How the documents came into the possessions of Bill Nelson would never be solved.

A Texas attorney who had represented Bill Nelson in the case that sent him to prison disclosed that Bill and Omaima had visited him in Laredo in early November. "She said she was from a wealthy family and she spoke French and English and sixteen dialects of Arabic."

William Nelson's record indicated that he had been a military pilot who later flew narcotics and stolen electronics across the Mexico-Texas border. His plane had been shot down twice by Mexican authorities. Detectives also discovered that Nelson had been previously married. His estranged wife had filed for divorce while Nelson was in prison, but it had never been finalised. So his marriage to Omaima had not been legal.

Meanwhile, Omaima Nelson asked again to talk to a psychiatrist. She ultimately spoke to two. One psychiatrist learned of even more depravity. Omaima told him that her husband was sexually assaulting her in their home on November 30th, 1991, when she reached for a pair of scissors, stabbed him, and then "freaked out." She followed up the stabbing by beating him with a steam iron until he was dead.

Before Omaima started to mutilate Nelson's body, the psychiatrist said, she put on red lipstick, a red hat, and red high-heeled shoes. She explained that she was fascinated with the colour of her husband's blood and wore red to make her butchery into a kind of ritual. She worked at her savage task all night.

Detective Phillips thought he had heard everything, but when he heard the next part of the doctor's report, even he was shocked. Omaima Nelson had admitted to the psychiatrist that she ate part of Bill Nelson's ribs after cooking them in barbecue sauce! The psychiatrist quoted Omaima's words: "I barbecued his ribs just like in a restaurant. I was sitting at the kitchen table and I remember saying to myself 'It's so sweet, it's so delicious, I like him tender.'"

In his diagnosis of Omaima Nelson, the psychiatrist said, "I believe she is psychotic." In his 20 years of practice, he had never seen anything so bizarre.

Another psychiatrist also concluded that Omaima was psychotic. She told him that she hacked off Nelson's genitals, and stuffed them in his mouth along with his left ring finger. Omaima said she removed the finger because Nelson "always came home and instead of kissing me hello, he would take his finger and shove it in me ... I hated that so much. It hurt, and it hurt my feelings so much. Why couldn't he just be nice?" If Omaima's story were true, she had rearranged the victim's body parts before wrapping them in newspaper and foil.

The trial of Omaima Nelson started on December 3rd, 1992, one year after her arrest.

In Prosecutor Randy Pawloski's opening statement, he told the jury that this would be the "ghastliest" story they would ever hear.

"In the next few weeks, you're going to hear a Rod Serling *Twilight Zone* type of thing."

He disputed Omaima's self-defence claim, arguing that it was William Nelson who was tied to the bed and stabbed, not Omaima. William was then clubbed into unconsciousness with an iron and dismembered, Pawloski informed the horrified jurors. "The evidence will show that we got a predator, we got evil, we got a mean peson who goes from guy to guy."

Omaima's wounds, the prosecutors suggested, had occurred during her wild frenzy of chopping up Bill Nelson's body.

Defence Attorney Tom Mooney told the jury that Omaima was the victim of a domineering man who had attacked her several times. She finally lashed back in self-defence, Mooney said. "She was reacting to years of abuse by other people ... She was out of it at the time and didn't know what she was doing. Mrs. Nelson is, and was that night, psychotic. Omaima will testify and tell the true story of what happened that night."

On December 9th a tearful Omaima Nelson took the stand and admitted killing and dismembering her husband, but she claimed she had done this to stop his continual abuse. He had raped her on Thanksgiving Day, she testified. Then he knocked her to the floor, ordered her to strip, and tied her up naked on the bed. When she couldn't stop crying, she said, he cut her breast with a knife and got on top of her. To protect herself, she grabbed a pair of scissors and started stabbing him. She then found the iron. "I hit him," she testified. "I broke the iron."

During her two days on the stand, Omaima also told jurors that because of the painful mutilating circumcision she had endured at the age of six, she had never been able to enjoy sex. (Excision of the clitoris and surrounding tissue, without the benefit of anaesthesia, is still a common practice in some African countries.)

Cross-examined by Pawloski, Omaima admitted that she had told a boy friend that she had been hoping to make a lot of money, maybe $50,000, so she could return to Egypt and start a business.

Pawloski also showed her a photograph of herself taken 24 hours after she claimed that Nelson had beaten her savagely. The photo revealed no bruises or injuries. Finally, with a touch of sarcasm, Pawloski said that investigators had not yet found all of the "meat" of Bill Nelson.

"We're missing about one hundred and thirty pounds of Bill," Pawloski growled. He then spun towards Omaima. "You know where he might have gone?" he asked.

The prosecutor pointed out that the remains of Bill Nelson's legs, chopped off at the knees, were bruised around the ankles, indicating that he had been bound during a struggle just before death. The headboard of the bed had also been broken, Pawloski said, showing that Nelson had struggled hard for his life.

Omaima Nelson was a "predator," the prosecutor insisted, who killed Bill Nelson so that she could flee with his money, credit cards, and the new red Corvette.

Defence Attorney Mooney reiterated that Omaima was "an ill woman," who was not guilty of premeditated murder.

Following six days of deliberation, the jury returned with their verdict. They found Omaima Nelson not guilty of first-degree murder, but they convicted her of second-degree murder. They had decided there was insufficient evidence of premeditation to support a first-degree murder conviction. Omaima Nelson was also found guilty of assaulting Orville Whittaker in November 1990.

Detective Bob Phillips commented: "Omaima Nelson is the most bizarre and sick individual I've ever had the occasion to meet. No one needs to look to the Dahmers of Milwaukee or the Hannibal Lecters of the screen. A new predator has emerged named Omaima."

On March 12th, 1992, Judge Robert Fitzgerald sentenced Omaima Aref Nelson to the maximum possible prison term, 27 years to life. She will not be eligible for parole until well into the 21st century.

But Omaima is not the only woman to have beheaded her victim . . .

2
HUMAN SACRIFICE

Bill Kelly

Sherri sat helpless, her wrists handcuffed behind her back

FOR 35-year-old Sherri Dally, the day started ordinarily enough. Deciding to do a little shopping before returning to her day-care business, she left her home on Channel Drive in Ventura, California, and at 9.30 a.m. she eased her white Dodge van onto the car park of the Target discount store on East Main Street.

But when noon arrived on that Monday, May 6th, 1996, and she hadn't returned home or phoned, her sister-in-law became so worried that she got in her car and went looking for her. Sherri, the beautiful mother of two sons, was a responsible person, as everyone knew. She was never away long from the business she ran from her home, and she never failed to pick her boys up from school.

Her sister-in-law drove the streets of Ventura, stopping briefly at every place where she thought Sherri might be. Finally she drove to the Target store where she knew Sherri sometimes shopped. Sherri wasn't there, but her van was. It wasn't locked and a bag of purchases was on the front seat. More alarming, a set of car and house keys lay on the floor next to her purse and her driving licence. The sister-in-law searched the mall, but there was no sign of her. Sherri had vanished.

Now even more anxious, the sister-in-law drove straight home and phoned Sherri's husband at the supermarket which he managed at Oxnard.

Michael Dally anxiously called the authorities around midnight, wanting to file a missing person report on his wife of 14 years. He explained that she hadn't returned home from shopping, but he was told there was a 72-hour waiting period before anyone could be listed missing. Nevertheless, at Dally's insistence the officer who took the call noted Sherri's description.

In the meantime Michael phoned Sherri's friends and relatives, but none had seen her. Since everyone knew that the couple were having matrimonial problems, many thought Sherri might have committed suicide. When that possibility was ruled out because of her strong ties with her children, they feared she had been abducted.

In the Dally family nobody slept that night. Michael enlisted a few friends and relatives to help him search the streets, and as days passed with still no sign of Sherri, Michael and his helpers prepared posters with her photo and description, distributing more than 3,000 throughout the area.

"I'm lost without my sweetheart," Dally told a reporter. But on May 14th, eight days after Sherri's disappearance, he did a strange thing. It seemed that he suspected his wife had simply run off, because he petitioned the Ventura County Superior Court for legal separation and full custody of his two sons. He said he was concerned about Sherri's state of mind and the possibility that she might abduct the children and he'd never see them again.

Stranger still, he phoned a charity shop and disposed of all Sherri's clothes. Friends visiting his home noticed that although there were photos on the walls of Michael and his two sons, there were none of his willowy blonde wife. A niece found Sherri's photos torn to bits in the dustbin.

Media reports of Sherri's disappearance prompted a man to come forward. He told the police he was having breakfast in his truck outside the Target store on May 6th when he saw what appeared to be an arrest taking place in the car park. Two blonde women were involved, he told detectives. One in a tan suit turned the other woman around, handcuffed her wrists and shoved her into the back seat of a blue-green Nissan Altima car. As it drove off he noticed it had rental plates.

From photos he identified the handcuffed woman as Sherri. She did not resist, he said, and the other woman "handcuffed her just like an officer would. I figured she was being arrested for shoplifting."

Investigators traced the Nissan Altima to an Oxnard rental agency and impounded it. A security camera had pictures of a woman, seemingly in a blonde wig, picking up the car. Several blonde hairs were found on the front and back seats, but the hairs in the front of the car were not human: they were from a wig. Splashes of blood were discovered on the back seat, the ceiling and on the interior side of a rear door, and someone had tried unsuccessfully to clean blood from the floor with a solvent.

The agency's records showed that the car had been rented by a Ms. Diana J. Haun, who turned out to be employed on the delicatessen counter at the supermarket managed by Michael Dally. It transpired that the couple's love affair had long been a source of gossip for their colleagues, and Sherri Dally had not been blind to the situation.

On May 18th detectives searched Diana Haun's flat at Port Hueneme and Dally's house in Ventura. Taken to police headquarters, the pair were questioned separately. Diana admitted that she and her boss were lovers, but Dally denied it.

Claiming she'd had no involvement in Sherri's disappearance, Diana Haun said that on the morning of May 6th she had been sunbathing on a beach. She had not witnesses, but without a body the police felt they had no option but to release her.

Another search for Sherri was organised by more than

100 of her friends and neighbours on May 25th. They found nothing, but a further search on June 1st revealed the skull, spine and other bones of a woman lying at the bottom of a ravine off Canada Larga Road between Ventura and Ojai.

The corpse had evidently been ravaged by coyotes and other animals known to frequent the area. They had been drawn to the spot, it was reported, by the decaying body's rank, pervasive odour.

Dental records established that the remains were those of Sherri Dally, and pathologist Ronald O'Halloran found that she had been killed by blunt force injuries to her head and at least 15 stab wounds to her upper torso, probably inflicted with a double-bladed knife or dagger.

The pathologist said that marks on the neck-bone and the underside of the skull suggested that Sherri had been beheaded by her attacker, probably with an axe.

On the following day police checking local wig shops called at Oxnard Discount Wigs and Beauty Supplies. Shown a photo of Diana Haun, an assistant identified her as a customer who had come into the shop on May 4th to buy a blonde wig.

"She said she wanted to play a trick on somebody," the assistant recalled. And after trying on the wig she had turned to him and asked if she looked as if she had "authority."

When she paid for the wig by cheque he noticed in her wallet the photo of Michael Dally and his sons that he had since seen on television.

On June 10th the police were recreating the abduction scene in a roped-off section of the Target car park when they were approached by a woman. She told them she was walking into the store on May 6th when she noticed a teal-coloured Nissan nearby with what seemed to be modified licence-plates. The driver appeared to be wearing a blonde wig and her heavy pancake make-up looked like a disguise. The witness said that the woman's odd appearance had prompted her to ask a security guard if the store had been held up . . .

By now more than 30 officers were involved in the Ventura police department's largest-ever murder investigation. On June 18th detectives again searched the homes of the two suspects. At Diana Haun's apartment they removed a typewriter to see if it had been used to produce an anonymous letter received by a local newspaper. The letter claimed that Sherri Dally's death was the work of British nationalists trying to embarrass the local police.

Protesting her innocence, Diana Haun was arrested on August 1st, and 15 days later she was indicted on charges of murder and kidnapping. Michael Dally's arrest followed on November 15th, when he too was indicted on murder and kidnapping charges. Additional charges of killing for financial gain and lying in wait meant that the couple could face the death penalty. They were to be tried separately.

A background check on Diana Haun established that she had been born in 1961, the daughter of a Pearl Harbor veteran and his Japanese bride. She had been an outstanding student, but at high school she had been severely injured when a basketball backboard collapsed, striking her head. In a coma for three days and having suffered a brain haemorrhage, she had received $1,077 a month from an insurance settlement until she collected Social Security.

She had nevertheless continued to do well academically, but on leaving school she had taken a series of humdrum jobs before she became a night-shift worker on the delicatessen counter at the supermarket where she fell in love with Michael Dally in December 1993.

During coffee breaks he informed her his marriage was on the rocks. She told detectives that once she was convinced he was no longer in love with his wife, they began an affair that took them from motel to motel over a period of seven months. She wrote Dally sexy love-letters, pledging her body to him in any way he wanted. Then Dally moved in with her, but five months later he returned to his home, saying he did not want to leave his sons alone with their unstable mother.

The investigators learned that Diana Haun had told colleagues that she was involved in witchcraft. One said, "She told me she cast a spell on a check-out girl and it was successful because the lady went on leave of absence.

"She said she was planning to perform a human sacrifice. I didn't have any idea what she was talking about and just nodded. She seemed to want to tell me something. She said something like she was going to sacrifice an unwanted person to celebrate a good friend's birthday, because that was the greatest proof of love there is. I thought she was just a bit mad."

Other employees at the supermarket told detectives that Dally not only cheated on his wife with Diana but also on his mistress with other women, including a prostitute. How did they know? He had bragged about it.

Ventura County Superior Court fell silent on June 30th when Diana Haun entered handcuffed and sat at the defence table in a beige jacket, black shirt and low-heeled shoes.

Deputy District Attorney Michael Frawley told the jury of the $50,000 insurance policy Dally had taken out on his wife, and discussions he'd had with a mistress he knew before he met Diana. He had spoken of pushing his wife off a cliff, running over her with a car — anything to get rid of her.

The prosecutor went on to say that the jury would hear that Michael Dally was the only man Sherri ever loved. They would hear how she tried to save her marriage although for years she knew her husband was unfaithful. Diana Haun, the jury would learn, had wanted to take Sherri's place so much that she carried a photo of Dally and his sons in her wallet. Sherri had been torn out of the picture.

"I'm going to tell you a little bit about Diana Haun," Michael Frawley continued. "You're going to learn that Michael and Diana used a code name for Sherri. In letters written back and forth they called her 'Alex.'"

He said that Diana had aspired to be a model, had taken acting courses, had a few bit-parts in movies, and used those skills to pose as a store detective to kidnap Sherri. Her interests also included black magic, and she had spoken of planning a human sacrifice as a boy friend's birthday treat. Michael Dally's birthday was May 21st, just two weeks after his wife vanished.

Diana was so obsessed with Dally, said Frawley, that she even obtained someone else's divorce papers, altered them to reflect the "divorce" of Sherri and Michael, and gave them to Dally as a Christmas present.

As for physical evidence, said the prosecutor, the state had plenty. There was the receipt for a camping hatchet used to cut off Sherri's head; there was the blood — proved by DNA testing to be Sherri's — in Diana's rented car; and there were the scratches and bruises on Diana's face and arms that she took to work on May 7th, evidence of Sherri's desperate fight for her life. And then there were the cheques showing that Diana had bought handcuffs, a security badge, a tan suit and a blonde wig only days before the murder.

Frawley then used a mannequin to show the jury what Diana looked like in her disguise.

On that fatal Monday morning, he said, Diana waited in the rented Nissan for Sherri to finish her shopping. Posing as a security guard, she tricked Sherri into submitting to being handcuffed before being taken to police head-quarters. But instead of heading for the police station, Diana had driven to Canada Larga Road where she stopped the car and beat and stabbed Sherri who was helpless in her handcuffs.

Deputy Public Defender Neil Quinn, however, por-trayed Diana Haun as a blameless, love-struck dupe, a non-violent vegetarian whose gullibility allowed Michael Dally to draw her into his plan to kill his wife because a divorce would leave him broke.

"She was blinded by love for Michael Dally," Quinn told the jury. "She was duped into Michael's plans. She makes a wrong decision, she clings to her man ..."

The handcuffs and other items she had bought, the defence claimed, had been purchased for Dally. And in an effort to ridicule one of the prosecution's props Quinn took the sunglasses off the mannequin dressed to resemble Diana's disguise and put them on himself. Diana never wore sunglasses, he claimed, unless she was on the beach.

Concluding his opening statement, the defence attorney asked the jury to acquit Diana because she never knew she was part of a murder plan. He claimed that she was not the killer, suggesting that a man who had used her credit card at a petrol-station had been involved with Michael Dally in the murder conspiracy.

The prosecution then called their first witness, a former girl friend of Michael Dally. A petite, attractive brunette, she told how she met Dally while working at a supermarket in Santa Barbara. Their sex sessions took place at her flat in Goleta, Dally sometimes phoning his wife to say he was too tired to drive home to Ventura and was spending the night with a colleague.

The witness went on to say that the first signs of Dally's darker side came when Sherri became pregnant. He became sullen and moody, complaining that Sherri had become pregnant because he wanted to end their marriage. Later he began talking of killing her. "He wanted her to disappear," said the witness. "There were times he talked about stabbing her with a knife, but not only stabbing her, but twisting the knife to cause pain."

The brunette went on to say she became nervous of Dally after a row. Some time ago he had told her that once he tried to lure Sherri to the cliffs at Big Sur. He said he could push her off making it look like an accident.

"After our row he suggested we take a day trip to the cliff area. I thought no way, you're not getting rid of me like that. I ended the affair there and then."

The witness said that Dally had already tried to choke her and only eased up when she begged him to stop and cried that she loved him.

During the time that Dally lived with Diana, the court was told, Sherri struggled desperately to save her marriage and was extremely depressed. A relative testified: "Sherri felt she had done everything she could to be a good wife and mother and couldn't understand why that wasn't enough." While her husband was living with Diana, Sherri had taken his clothes home with her, returning them washed and ironed. She had also collected Michael's car, washed it, and returned it to Diana's apartment.

"My God, why do you do it?" the relative had asked Sherri.

"Because I love him so much," she'd replied.

The witness said that Dally never missed a meal. "If he was going to work at two a.m., Sherri got up to cook for him. If he needed to eat at four a.m., she was up at three a.m. She always felt she was not worthy of him."

During one confrontation with Diana, Sherri had told her she would get Michael over her dead body.

A detective told the court that Diana's phone records showed that on May 6th she had made several calls to Dally and to a dry cleaner's. The owner of the cleaners testified that Diana had phoned asking about removing blood from car upholstery. The prosecutor said she had decided to use cleaning fluids instead.

The court then heard the evidence of a prostitute who said that she and several other hookers frequently serviced Dally. While she was in jail on a drugs charge she had told Diana that Michael was a frequent client.

The prostitute went on to say that while she and Dally were smoking rock cocaine and having sex in the summer of 1996, Dally told her that his wife was dead. "He was non-feeling. I remember watching his face and there was nothing."

Another witness told the jury that at about 2.30 p.m. on May 6th he had seen a blonde driving a blue-green car along Canada Larga Road, near the ravine where Sherri's dismembered remains were found a month later.

In her closing argument for the prosecution Lela

Henke-Dobroth recalled the horror at the ravine in Canada Larga Road. Diana had pulled in a parking area right beside the ravine. The car park was empty and nobody was around. Taking the knife from the back of the vehicle she opened the rear door. Sherri sat helpless, her wrists handcuffed behind her back. In a frenzy Diana stabbed Sherri in the chest several times. She slumped forward, falling from the car. Diana returned to the boot and fetched an axe. After hacking at her victim then chopping the head off she rolled the remains over the edge into the ravine for wild animals to ravage.

The six-week trial ended on September 26th, 1997, when after nearly five hours' deliberation the jury convicted 36-year-old Diana Haun of first-degree murder, kidnapping, conspiracy to commit murder, and murder for financial gain. Judge Frederick A. Jones then ordered the jury to return on October 28th to recommend whether she should be put to death or sentenced to life without parole. The prosecutors intimated that they would try to persuade her to testify against Dally in a deal to drop the death penalty.

"I think it's human nature to save her own life, even though there must have been a very strong love between her and Dally," commented an attorney who had followed the trial closely.

Diana Haun was subsequently spared execution, the jury deciding she had been Dally's pawn in his murder scheme. The judge turned down a request for reduced time in prison in exchange for her testimony against Dally, and she was sentenced to life without parole.

Michael Dally was asked by a reporter if he loved her. "Love?" he replied. "Yes, you could call it that."

At his subsequent trial he denied plotting to kill his wife. He claimed he had no idea that Diana Haun had stabbed Sherri to death and hidden her body. His lawyers argued that Diana had acted alone out of her obsession with her lover.

But on April 6th Michael Dally was found guilty of first-degree murder, kidnapping, conspiracy and lying in wait, the prosecutors announcing they would seek the death penalty. After three days' deliberation, however, on Friday April 24th, 1998, the jury declared themselves hopelessly deadlocked seven to five in favour of the death sentence. In view of this the prosecutors said they would no longer press for the death penalty. They would settle for life imprisonment without parole. On hearing this, 37-year-old Dally smiled and embraced his attorneys.

It transpired that his life had been saved by his two sons, aged eight and ten. For the jurors who had voted for life imprisonment revealed they had felt unable to recommend death because of its potential impact on his children.

Even so, said a friend of Sherri expressing her sympathy for the two sons, "it's got to be kind of hard knowing your dad's girl friend axed mom."

Americans were shocked by the viciousness of Diana Haun's crime... Meanwhile in Britain...

3

ROAD RAGE

Brian Marriner

***The public held its breath... was she
guilty or was she telling the truth?***

ONCE IN A while there is a murder trial that rivets the
whole nation, a courtroom drama on everone's lips.
That's how it was in the case of Tracie Andrews. There
was no doubting her sultry beautry... but was it just skin-
deep? Was she a beautiful killer? She emphatically denied
murdering her boy friend, but would the jury believe her?

On the night of December 1st, 1996, a woman solicitor
was watching TV at her Worcestershire home with a
friend. It was 10.50 p.m. when he left. Stepping into the
lane outside — Coopers Hill, near Alvechurch — he heard
the frantic voice of a woman asking him to call an
ambulance.

He returned inside, asked his host to dial 999, and then
went out into the lane again where he saw the young
woman standing by the part-open door of a Ford Escort.
She was covered with blood, shaking and apparently in
shock. The body of a young man lay in the road nearby.
Asked if there had been a traffic accident, the young
woman said, "No." The man who had gone to her
assistance had not heard another vehicle drive away.

When the two were joined by the householder who had

dialled 999 the young woman spoke of a road rage attack. She had more to say when the police arrived. By then her story was complete and fluent.

Tracie Andrews, a 27-year-old single mother, said that as she and her live-in lover Lee Harvey were driving home from a night out at the Marlbrook Inn on the outskirts of Bromsgrove they were followed for several miles by two men in a dark-coloured F-registered saloon car, possibly a Ford Sierra. It had been a "cat and mouse" chase, she said. They were eventually overtaken and forced to stop. A big man — the passenger — got out of the pursuing car and attacked Lee Harvey, mistakenly calling him a "Paki bastard," shouting obscenities and stabbing him repeatedly with a knife, before turning his rage on Tracie.

Tracie Andrews gave a detailed description of the assailant, adding that during the fight his companion had called him "Jez." Since she had several cuts and bruises to her face, she was taken by ambulance to hospital where she spent three hours being treated for her injuries. During this time she made several trips to the lavatory alone, on one occasion spending so long there that the ward sister banged on the door to ask if she was all right.

Meanwhile at 3.20 a.m. the doorbell rang at the detached home of Lee Harvey's parents in King's Norton, Birmingham. They thought that maybe their son had forgotten his keys and wanted to spend the night with them, perhaps following a row with Tracie. But it was the police calling to notify them of the death of their 25-year-old son, who had received more than 30 stab wounds.

By the next day detectives had taken a statement from Tracie and were conducting house-to-house enquiries, as well as a finger-tip search of the immediate area of the attack. They were puzzled by the lack of any apparent motive for the crime, and speculated that it might be connected with a drugs deal gone wrong. A Photofit picture was assembled from Tracie Andrews's description and circulated to the press.

As was routine in such cases, inquiries were also made

into the backgrounds of the victims, and the picture which emerged gave the investigators something else to think about. They learned that the couple were always fighting. In a nightclub Tracie Andrews had been seen to bite Lee's neck during a row. And a police officer on late-night patrol had at one time come across the couple scuffling. He saw Tracie trying to strike Lee Harvey, who was attempting to placate her.

After a search of the murder scene had revealed some tell-tale clues, witnesses were found who had driven along the same road that night and had seen the white Escort RS 2000 — without any road-rage vehicle following.

Tracie Andrews was now the prime suspect, but she was nevertheless encouraged to appear on TV as a grieving victim, and through her tears beg the public to help find the killer of the man she loved. The police have been known to use such TV appeals as an investigative weapon, hoping the suspects will trip themselves up while on camera.

Tracie Andrews duly made her emotional broadcast, eyes red from weeping and face contorted with grief. It was not long after this — six days after a suicide attempt, in fact — that she was arrested and charged with Lee Harvey's murder. But as the evidence was all circumstantial, she was allowed bail right up to and throughout her trial.

The West Mercia Police investigation had been exhaustive.

Lee Harvey was a handsome bus driver with a nice car and a steady job. A bachelor, he had a child from a teenage affair, still keeping in touch with the mother of his daughter. With his dark good looks he had vague aspirations to become a male model, but he never did anything about it. From an early age he wanted only to be a lorry driver like his father. After leaving school at 16 he had worked for his uncle for a while before getting the bus driving job. He appeared to be very laid-back, going to the local nightclub every weekend and having plenty of girl friends. But beneath the veneer of "Joe Cool" he was vulnerable, someone who could be easily exploited because all he wanted was a settled home life with the right woman. When he met Tracie Andrews he thought he had found Mrs. Right.

She had lived with another man for a couple of years, bearing his child. But 10 months after her daughter's birth the relationship crumbled and she had moved out, eventually getting a council flat and supplementing the maintenance she was receiving by working in the beauty products business and behind the bar at two hotels. At weekends she was to be found in the disco bars in Birmingham's Broad Street. Then she spotted Lee Harvey.

Six weeks after meeting Lee in Ritzy's nightclub in Birmingham in 1994 she asked him to move into her flat in Alvechurch. There were frequent rows and simmering discontents.

Some years before, she had set up home with another man. She had once brandished a knife at him during a row, and the police interviewed him about this during their investigation. He said that a row developed as they drove from a night out at a pub, Tracie complaining that he shouldn't be driving after drinking. He explained he had only had one pint. He went on: "When we got home Tracie flipped. She took a knife from the kitchen and waved it towards me. She had lost it. I took the knife from her hand and grabbed it. When Tracie gets angry her eyes go wide."

Prior to her trial her solicitors held a press conference to announce that they had uncovered fresh evidence. Tracie Andrews appeared before the assembled pressmen, watching her solicitor appeal for new witnesses to come forward. Sitting at her back, uninvited, was the police officer in charge of the murder inquiry.

Tracie's solicitor, Mr. Robinson, said: "A mature lady social worker has provided us with details of a road rage incident in the same general area some weeks before the date of the murder." He said the description she gave of her attacker bore "a remarkable likeness to the passenger in the car which overtook and stopped Miss Andrews and Mr. Harvey."

He added that other witnesses had also come forward. "The police were unable to unearth this information, and yet it has taken us only six weeks to do so."

The police officer said afterwards that nothing he had heard would cause him to alter the course of his investigation, although he would always keep an open mind. A top lawyer commented that holding press conferences prior to a trial was a tactic increasingly being used by defence teams. It helped counter-balance the bad publicity of the arrest.

Finally, Tracie Andrews stepped into the glass-screened dock in Court Nine at Birmingham Crown Court on July 1st, 1997, to plead not guilty to murder. Smartly dressed, her long blonde hair carefully waved, she listened impassively to Mr. David Crigman QC, prosecuting, as he made his opening speech to the jury.

He said that her story of a road rage attack was complete fiction. She had been able to give the police such a detailed account because she had been involved in a similar incident previously, and had used the circumstances of that — and the face of a man she had seen briefly in a pub — to produce her scenario.

Mr. Crigman said that Tracie Andrews had stabbed Lee Harvey more than 30 times with a Swiss Army-style knife. She then tucked it in one of her boots, hiding it in a rubbish bin in a toilet. By the time police had identified her as the culprit, the bin's contents had been thrown away.

Holding up the right size-four boot, the prosecutor told the jury that a forensic scientist examining the lining had found a bloodstain near the top. It was just over two and a half inches long and one inch wide and could have been made by contact with a blood-wetted object slid into the boot. Analysis showed that the stain had a DNA content consistent with having come from Lee Harvey.

Three human hairs found in the victim's right hand matched those of Tracie Andrews. And a whole hank of hair matching that of the defendant had been ripped from her scalp by Mr. Harvey as he defended himself. Mr. Crigman said: "When police questioned her about this, she said her hair came out easily. This hank of hair, says the Crown, has been hauled from her scalp, roots and all."

Describing the couple's "turbulent and volatile" relationship, Mr. Crigman said they met in 1993 and a relationship developed the following year when Mr. Harvey, who had previously lived with his parents, moved in with Tracie Andrews and her daughter.

When the couple argued Lee Harvey would sometimes move out of the flat in Alvechurch and return to his parents' home until things cooled down. Then he would go back to the flat until the next time. On one occasion the police were called to the flat where they found Tracie standing amid broken electronic equipment. She complained that Lee had thrown a portable television set and video cassette at her. The two officers gave advice and left.

Mr. Crigman said that on the day Mr. Harvey died witnesses had seen the couple at the Marlbrook Inn. They "were not overtly arguing in public but gave the impression that they were ill at ease with each other." It was on their homeward journey, Mr. Crigman claimed, that Tracie Andrews killed her boy friend in a frenzy of rage.

"It was a late-night crime in a quiet lane for which not only was no weapon found but there were no eye-witnesses. But the Crown will produce evidence relating to the couple's homeward journey which proves unequivocally that the road-rage story is untrue," said the prosecutor.

He read out the statement made by Tracie Andrews to the police. She had bruises and cuts to her left eye and the bridge of her nose, Mr. Crigman said, but "these injuries were caused by Lee Harvey in what was to be their final and fatal confrontation ...

"There was no other car. There was not some mysterious, murderous motorist. It was her."

The couple had an argument as they drove home, and stopped, the prosecutor continued. At some point during the 12 to 15-minute journey Mr. Harvey hit his girl friend, causing her facial injuries. Although they knew the road well, they overshot the Coopers Hill junction and reversed to turn into it. Some distance along the lane Lee Harvey pulled up and both of them left the vehicle.

"It is the case of the Crown that this defendant launched a most vicious attack on Mr. Harvey," said Mr. Crigman. The victim had been stabbed "predominantly to the neck, to the face, to the back of his head, left side of the body, left shoulder and in the back. It is likely that the attack continued after he collapsed to the ground and abated only as her anger subsided.

"The ferocity of the attack on the boy friend and the area where the attack was concentrated, namely the neck, would have quickly rendered Lee Harvey defenceless. Both the carotid artery and the jugular vein were severed. It would have led to the immediate and massive spurting of blood pouring from his neck. No doubt he would have tried to move away from her, but he could not have moved far before collapsing on the ground and dying."

As the jury were shown photographs of Lee's wounds, his mother burst into tears in the public gallery.

Mr. Crigman went on to describe how Tracie Andrews was first observed at the scene by the man who went to her assistance. "Was she tending the body of the man? No, she was not. Was she running to the house for help? No, she was not doing that either. She was standing by the driver's door with her back to the car and she was covered in blood." She did not mention another car at this point or refer to any road rage attack. It was only when the woman occupant of the cottage got to her side after dialling 999 that the road-rage story had its beginning."

The prosecutor said that some time after the murder, in

response to a police appeal for witnesses, a couple came forward with evidence which threw doubt on Tracie Andrews's story of the car chase. Two accountants from Bromsgrove driving that same stretch of road that night recalled seeing a white Escort with alloy wheels and a spoiler that corresponded with Mr. Harvey's car. Driving near Coopers Hill, they saw the Escort's headlights and watched as it overshot the turning into the lane and reversed.

"Their testimony is vital because the timing was right and so was the location," Mr. Crigman said. The couple told detectives that they saw no pursuing car, and despite driving one and a half miles along the road from which the Escort had travelled before turning off, they saw no sign of another vehicle going in either direction.

Concluding his opening speech, Mr. Crigman told the jury that Lee and Tracie "had another of their rows, a fierce row. She stabbed him and he pulled a clump of hair from the scalp of the person who was fighting him. His blood was spurting on to her jumper and he quickly died. From that moment, she has firmly lied."

The woman who had dialled 999 was a former detective constable, and she told the jury: "I had my suspicions of Andrews from the very start." These had been aroused because when the witness questioned her, Tracie had not described her fiancé's attacker or the car involved in the alleged road rage incident. Yet minutes later when the police arrived she gave them a description of a dark-coloured Ford Sierra and described the attacker in some detail.

The former policewoman, now a solicitor, testified that Tracie Andrews had told her that she and Mr. Harvey had been to a pub where there had been an argument with another man. "She said Lee had cut one of these men up but had stopped the car and shouldn't have. She told him not to get out, but he did."

Mr. Crigman asked the witness if she had heard any other car speeding away that night. She replied: "I heard absolutely nothing."

The witness had taken Tracie Andrews into the kitchen of her cottage just yards from the scene of the crime. She told the court: "What she was saying seemed very disjointed at the time. I asked her about the other vehicle, if she had seen the colour of it. She said no. I asked if she had seen its make. She said no. I asked if there was any part of the registration number she could remember. She said no and there was nothing about the car she could recall.

"I asked about the men, if she knew them. She said no. I asked her if she had ever seen these men before and she replied no. I asked her if she had heard any names being used by these men. She said no." The witness said she had drawn on her 10 years' police experience and her legal training to form her questions. "I thought it was vital they were asked. Had she been able to tell me the answers I could have given them to the police and they could have got on with their investigation sooner."

A police officer had arrived then at the witness's home and started asking Tracie Andrews questions. "I heard her tell the police the other car was a black Sierra. She was also adamant that the person responsible for assaulting Mr. Harvey was the passenger, and she described him. I thought it was strange, and I believe I remarked upon it to the officer."

Mr. Ronald Thwaites QC, defending, put it to the witness that she had not mentioned her questioning of the defendant in her first statement. It was only after Tracie Andrews had been charged with murder that she added the story in a subsequent statement three days later, he said. The witness replied that she thought she had mentioned the questioning, but she might have been distracted while making her statement.

She described how she found Mr. Harvey lying in the road with his throat apparently cut. Tracie was standing behind the Ford Escort, distressed and crying, with blood all over her face. She went up to Mr. Harvey's body at least twice and said something which the witness couldn't hear.

The prosecution then turned to the statement the defendant had made to the police. She had told detectives that she and Lee often argued but were deeply in love. They had become engaged in 1995.

"We have had our arguments and split up a few times when Lee would go back to his parents' house, but we always got back together."

She said she did not realise Lee had been stabbed until she saw blood on her hands as she cradled his dead body.

But in that police interview she had been unable to explain discrepancies in her description of the murder. She said the fight took place in front of the car — the blood was found at its rear. Told that two witnesses had seen the couple's car near the murder scene but had not observed any other vehicle following it, she was asked to explain this and replied simply: "I can't." Nor could she explain why, if she had stayed in the car, Lee's blood had spurted on to the front of her jumper.

The defence counsel now sought to show Tracie Andrews in a different light, while besmirching the character of the victim. He told the jury that Tracie Andrews was an ordinary woman wrongly accused of committing an horrendous crime. He said that his client had been vilified as a "wicked person," effectively convicted before one word of her defence had been heard. She had been cast as a "horror movie monster," and despite having led a blameless life was being cast as the "demon from hell."

"Tracie Andrews did not have a motive for murder," said Mr. Thwaites, "she had a motive for marriage. This is the man she had fixed upon and he upon her ... they had found glamour with each other, charm with each other, they wanted each other." She had worn his engagement ring on the night he was killed, and she was still wearing it now as she was tried for his murder.

The defence counsel said it would be extraordinary for a young woman to spend an evening in a pub with her lover, only for it to end in such an "horrendous blood-bath in the road." Although the couple's relationship had its "ups and downs," these were caused by the dead man's inability to control his "obsessional" jealousy. He could not cope with the fact that his lover had a child from a previous relationship, and he tried to control her life by monitoring her movements and banning her from seeing even girl friends.

But Tracie, said Mr. Thwaites, was a "sensible, level-headed, practical young woman of the Nineties who could cope with her life and with her young daughter."

The victim, said the defence counsel, was a pathetic and immature man who could not cope with life and whose jealous fits would lead to him being thrown out of the couple's home. But Tracie Andrews took him back "because she loved him." She had become pregnant by Mr. Harvey but, afraid that this would be a "burden he would not welcome," she'd had a termination, telling him she had miscarried. After her pregnancy she lost her figure and bust.

Mr. Harvey, after apologising for cruel comments he made about her body, had paid for her to have cosmetic breast surgery.

Describing Tracie Andrews as a "broken person" after her fiancé's death, Mr. Thwaites said she had tried to kill herself because of feelings of inadequacy over being unable to save his life.

The defence counsel said that reliable police informants had repeatedly identified a suspect matching Tracie Andrews's description of her fiancé's killer, but they were ignored by "blinkered detectives." The informers had said that they saw this suspect follow Lee Harvey out of the pub on the night he was killed. It was also claimed that the victim had been a drug dealer who knew the suspect "Mr. X," who had been involved in a similar road rage attack several years earlier.

Mr. Thwaites said that five days after the murder an anonymous caller telephoned the police to say he had seen

Mr. X leaving the pub after Lee Harvey. Mr. Thwaites read from the police log of the call, saying, "When Harvey left the pub he was followed by Mr. X, having had long eye contact as Harvey was going. It was thought they were going to fight, but Mr. X got into the passenger seat of a dark blue Ford Sierra."

An officer from the Regional Crime Squad had been given Mr. X's name on December 3rd, after receiving a call from an informant. The caller had told the detective that Mr. X was a drug dealer who was carrying a large amount of cocaine in the pub on the night of the murder. The informer's description of Mr. X was of "a fat man with piercing eyes" — matching Tracie Andrews's description of the attacker. Mr. Thwaites complained that the police had ignored this evidence, insisting on regarding Tracie Andrews as the prime suspect.

His vigorous defence of his client had turned the trial in her favour. All Britain asked: Was Tracie Andrews in fact telling the truth? Was Lee Harvey a victim of a road rage killer?

The drama heightened on July 14th, two weeks into the trial when Tracie Andrews went into the witness box to tell her own story, saying that after her boy friend's death she had attempted suicide. "I felt I had no future life. I loved Lee more than anything in the world." So she had taken approximately 200 tablets.

She said the only thing which gave her strength to carry on was her daughter. Pointing dramatically to the public gallery, she told the jury: "I want to come here one day. I want to sit there and I want to see the person who did this."

Asked to describe her relationship with Lee Harvey, she said it was "very, very loving and stormy at times." The storminess resulted from insecurity on both sides. But the fact that both she and Lee had children by previous relationships had "absolutely no effect" on her. She said she thought it was a good thing that they were both in the same situation and could "understand each other more."

Both she and Lee could be jealous, and both had a temper, but he showed his feelings much more than she did, she claimed. The second time they met he told her he had informed his family that he had met the woman he wanted to marry.

Her initial feelings were not as strong as Lee's, she said, but she came to love him and believed he loved her. His jealousy, however, had driven her to ask him to leave the home they had begun to share soon after meeting. She had a part-time job in a pub in Alvechurch and Lee would vet the outfits she wore to work, sometimes making her change before she went out to do her shift. He would insist on meeting her and walking her home when she went out with friends.

Describing the murder, she told the jury that Lee had been stabbed by a "porky man with big staring eyes who was wearing a donkey jacket." She went on: "He called Lee a Paki bastard. I saw the passenger strike out at Lee. I could not be sure how many times but it was more than once. Lee fell down on the floor and that's when I got out of the car."

She said the man was crouching over Lee but she could see no weapon. She swore at the man and he hit her. "He called me a slut and he punched me in the face. He hit me really hard and straightaway I fell. I remember tripping over Lee as I fell. I put my hands out and banged my head on the road."

She heard the driver of the other car call out: "Leave it, Jez," and the man got into the car and they both drove away. "When I got up I saw Lee lying in the road. I knelt down by him in something wet. He was making a funny noise — as though he was gurgling. I didn't know what to do. I was in a bad way myself."

While being asked about her love for the dead man, she left the witness box with the judge's permission and walked along in front of the jury to show them the engagement ring she still wore. On another occasion she paused mid-way through a sentence in which she was saying she only hit Lee in self-defence. She complained about remarks from the victim's family who were in the public gallery. "I'm sorry, but I can't put up with that while I'm giving evidence," she protested. Asked what had distracted her, she said: "The family are making remarks and it's not fair." Mr. Justice Buckley said he had not heard any remarks.

Continuing, she said that she wished Lee's murderer had killed her too. But when asked by her counsel to explain how hair pulled from her head was found in Lee's hand, she said she did not know how that had happened.

In calling his client to give evidence Mr. Thwaites was taking a risk, because this allowed the prosecution to cross-examine her. Had she not been called, the Crown would not have had that opportunity.

Questioning her, Mr. Crigman said: "This other car is a phantom. It doesn't exist, does it?"

"It does," Tracie Andrews insisted.

"Your relationship was always on the edge of some kind of explosion, wasn't it?" Mr. Crigman continued.

"Not always, no."

"Your evidence yesterday described the dangerous overtaking that occurred before Lee made a left hand turn in Burcot, but on the night of the murder you gave police an entirely different location. You have changed your story, haven't you, as a deliberate deceit?"

"I haven't. I just can't be sure. If anybody would have said there was a pink elephant in the road I would have said yes because of the state of mind I was in on that night."

"You have not invented a pink elephant but invented a black Sierra."

Tracie Andrews said she had invented nothing and had tried to help the police as best she could. She was to remain remarkably composed throughout two days of intensive cross-examination.

Mr. Crigman told her: "You and Lee had a row. You both stormed out of the car to the back of the car and you had an almighty set-to. In the course of it you got a penknife and you stabbed him time and time again."

"No, I did not."

"He was trying to get away from whoever was sticking the knife into him again and again. You were sticking a penknife into him as he retreated."

"No, I wasn't."

"You were stabbing him in the back in your anger and fury."

"There was no anger and no fury."

"You were in such a fury you just lashed out and lashed out and he tried to get away and you stabbed him in the back and when he fell over you stabbed him some more."

"No, I didn't."

Mr. Crigman said Tracie Andrews had told the police that the attack on Lee lasted 10 minutes. She had given different versions of the time they left the pub. The white Escort Lee was driving was spotted near Coopers Hill between 10.28 and 10.32 p.m. The first witness on the scene came out of the nearby cottage and saw the victim's body in the road at 10.50. That left a gap of about 17 minutes between the death of Lee and the witness leaving the cottage to get into his car.

"On your account the whole episode lasted ten minutes," the prosecutor told Tracie Andrews. "How do you explain the seven minutes after these alleged men have gone, but before the witness arrived?"

"I can't."

"What were you doing for fifteen, sixteen, seventeen minutes? For any of those seventeen minutes did you make the slightest attempt to alert the occupant of that house?"

"It wasn't until the light came on outside the house that I was able to shout for help ... Lee was lying on the ground. I did not want to leave him."

"If you didn't want to leave him, why didn't you put your hand on the horn?"

"I don't know."

"With a man with whom you have a relationship lying

immobile on the floor, you don't even shout to the house, let alone go to it?"

"No, I did not ... the man hit me very hard ... All I remember is running over to the car ... Everything to me is just like a dream ... I should have done a lot of things ... I was in shock."

"What you wanted outside that house, when you had come to the shocking realisation of what you had done, was some thinking time, wasn't it?" asked Mr. Crigman.

"No."

"If you were not guilty you would have been up that cottage drive like greased lightning."

"How does anybody know how they are going to react to a situation like this?" Tracie Andrews replied.

Mr. Crigman told her that her blood-soaked jumper proved she must have been "within one arm's length" of Lee when he was stabbed in the neck. He asked: "When could you have got blood that came out in a gush like a fountain from his carotid artery on your jumper?"

She replied: "I cannot answer that. I do not know."

Asked to explain how her hairs came to be found in Lee's hand, she said she could not remember him pulling it, but it was "very usual" for her hair to fall out because it was in bad condition from being bleached to remain blonde.

Mr. Crigman produced a Swiss Army penknife similar to the one with which he claimed she had stabbed Lee. He showed the jury how if it closed during an attack it would cut the assailant's little finger. Tracie Andrews had suffered such a wound.

"You are a woman of considerable deceit, aren't you, Miss Andrews?" the prosecutor continued.

"No, I am not."

"You were shocked at the realisation of how vicious your temper had become, weren't you?"

"I have not got a vicious temper."

Reminding Tracie Andrews of an incident in a nightclub when she bit Lee Harvey, Mr. Crigman asked: "What made a sensible, practical, level-headed young woman go for his neck with your teeth?"

Tracie Andrews claimed that Lee had grabbed her wrist and would not let go, and she had retaliated by biting him.

"When your teeth were in his neck, how did you feel?" asked Mr. Crigman.

"I was angry with him."

"It must require a real intensity of feeling to put your teeth into someone's neck. It's no mild emotion, is it?"

"People do things. Lee has done things to me."

"It was exactly the same intensity, but magnified by everything that followed, that led you to put a knife in his neck, wasn't it?"

"No."

Mr. Crigman reminded her of a road rage incident in which she had been involved in the company of a previous boy friend. He said this had taken place in Swan Street, Alvechurch, where she had lived previously. "You got involved in a fierce row with the driver of another car during which you drove off with him on your bonnet."

"No. I went into the back of the car and the driver came up to my window to have a go at me. The lad I was with was going to get out and have a word with him. The driver tried to stop me driving away."

Mr. Crigman persisted: "You had an ugly incident with another driver where there was a threat of violence. You drew on that."

"No."

The prosecutor said that Tracie Andrews had chosen an F-registered black Sierra for the car involved in Mr. Harvey's murder also from her own past experience. He said she had a black F-registered Ford Orion, owned by Mr. Harvey but registered in her name.

"That's just circumstantial," the defendant snapped.

"You invent people and then you introduce bits and pieces of your life experience," said Mr. Crigman.

He claimed that after killing Mr. Harvey near the cottage on Coopers Hill she had turned off the lights of their Ford Escort to give herself thinking-time. "In your statement you said the headlights were on, but the evidence of the police and the owner of the cottage is that the lights were off. Your blood mingled with Lee Harvey's was on the edge of the car door which you had pulled open further to switch off the lights. You wanted it dark for more thinking time. If anybody had looked out they would have seen the lights."

On the 13th day of the trial Mr. Mark Webster, a forensic scientist appearing for the defence, said that blood on Tracie Andrews's jumper could have sprayed from the victim's carotid artery as she fell across him. "If she fell facing him it's a possibility that arterial blood could have got on her jumper at that time. It could possibly be just one heart-beat's worth of blood."

Referring to Tracie Andrews's statement that as she cradled Mr. Harvey he was still breathing and "making gurgling noises," Mr. Webster suggested that the blood could have splashed onto her jumper at that time.

Turning to the blood found in the defendant's boot, Mr. Webster said that although the stain could have been made by a blood-wetted knife it could equally well have been left by thumb or finger. He added that blood might also have run into Tracie Andrews's boot from her trousers if they rode up above the top of her boots.

The defence then called a witness who was the defendant's former employer. She told the court that Tracie, whom she had known for about eight years, had often looked after her children. She was "loving and kind" with a "lovely temperament — she hasn't got a bad bone in her body."

Defence counsel asked her if she had ever seen any sign of temper in Tracie Andrews. "None. She is totally reliable, totally trustworthy."

Cross-examined by the prosecution, however, the witness was asked if she had been surprised by the evidence that Tracie Andrews had drawn blood by biting Lee Harvey's neck. "It did surprise me," the witness conceded.

Finally, a businesswoman who had employed Tracie Andrews for four and-a-half years in a perfume promotions role testified that the defendant was totally honest and would not lie on oath.

In his closing speech for the defence, Mr. Thwaites claimed that Tracie Andrews had become an innocent victim of police suspicion. He said that the police team had failed to follow up other lines of investigation properly. The superintendent had "put on the blinkers and he never looked back."

Mr. Thwaites said that at first the police had accepted Tracie Andrews's version of events. He said that her failure to remember accurately the route she and Lee took on the night of the murder was understandable, considering that she had seen her fiancé brutally murdered in front of her. Claims that she had hidden the murder weapon were pure speculation.

The jury, the defence counsel continued, had seen the small size of Tracie's hands. "How could she, with those little hands, have stabbed a man more than thirty times and only suffered one small cut to the edge of her little finger?"

Mr. Thwaites said the Crown had created a "myth" that she had a motive for murdering the man she intended to marry. But she was no "demon from hell" and had no possible motive for murdering the man she loved.

Mr. Crigman told the jury that a "formidable body of evidence" proved that Tracie Andrews killed her lover. "There are features of this case that we say incriminate this defendant in circumstances where no sensible or reasonable alternative explanation exists at all."

Summing-up, Mr. Justice Buckley told the jury they must decide whether Tracie Andrews was telling the truth. "You may feel that is what this case has really been about — consideration of all the circumstances to see if the defendant's account stands up. The defendant does not have to prove her account. The prosecution has to disprove it."

The trial had captured the public's attention like no other for many a year, and now that public held its breath. Would Tracie Andrews be convicted or acquitted? Argument for and against her replaced everyday banter in pubs and offices — which way would the verdict go?

On July 29th, 1997, the jury kept the nation guessing for five hours while they deliberated. Then they unanimously found Tracie Andrews guilty of murder. She shook her head in the dock when she heard the verdict, folding her arms defiantly and showing no emotion. An hour or so earlier she had told a reporter: "I know they are going to find me guilty of murder, but I didn't commit this terrible crime."

Before she was sentenced Mr. Thwaites said in mitigation that had she possessed "the courage to confront her own wrong-doing" from the start, the outcome of the case might have been different. He went on: "The court may wish to believe that the killing was the result of a spontaneous outburst of passion mixed with other powerful feelings that overwhelmed Miss Andrews and which she converted into deadly action. She may not have realised in the heat of the moment how many times she stabbed her fiancé. Today she can only wish she could turn the clock back. Lee Harvey has lost his life; the life of this woman is in ruins; she has a young daughter of just seven ..."

Tracie Andrews was then told by Mr. Justice Buckley: "The jury has found you guilty on very strong evidence of murder. Only you know precisely what went on that night, but we have all seen the awful consequences. Certainly it has been a tragedy for all concerned and I feel deeply for the families on both sides. As you know, there is only one sentence prescribed by law and that is life imprisonment."

In August solicitors for Tracie were reported to have found a vital new witness who had seen "the whole episode." This new evidence, it was reported, would form the basis of an appeal against conviction.

This was heard in the autumn of 1998, and the appeal was dismissed. But there were still those who believed her to be innocent... until April 1999, when she was reported to have confessed.

In a letter to a friend sent from Bullwood Hall Prison, Essex, she was reported to have admitted stabbing Lee Harvey during "a stupid fight that had got out of hand." The letter — subsequently published by the *News of the World* — said that as they drove home after an evening in a pub Mr. Harvey produced a knife and threatened "to slash my face or stab me."

They were having a row about her ex-lover, a man named Andy. They both got out of the car, Tracie Andrews claimed, and Mr. Harvey "came straight up to me and grabbed my hair. He said, 'See if Andy wants you with a f——d-up face.' He had a knife and I was scared. With that I kneed him. He fell down and pulled me down too. We fell over to the grass verge opposite the car. He hit me and I fell back.

"I got up and tried to hit him back. We was shouting at each other all the time. He punched me again. I fell. I saw the knife on the floor, picked it up, and when he went for me again I just reacted with the knife.

"I must have stabbed him. Then he stood still and shouted, 'You f——ing' bitch!' Then he hit me so hard I fell again. I got up halfway and all I can remember is seeing red. I just went mad... I was shaking and had lost all control. I have never ever in my life lost control like I did this night."

She recalled: "I went back over to Lee and tried talking, shaking him. I could hear him breathing in a bad way. I saw his eyes go to the back of his head. I could smell this awful smell and I felt the wetness on my hands."

Then as she cradled her dying boy friend at the roadside, she wrote, she felt sick. When she realised he was dead, she felt that her "whole life had ended."

The letter said: "I knew I had to make it look as though we had been attacked." So she slipped the knife down her trousers. "I went to the hospital. I flushed the knife down the toilet."

Regretting the false story she had told the police, she wrote: "I do feel I should have been convicted for manslaughter. I should have told the truth in the first place..."

But was she telling the truth now?

Relatives of Lee Harvey said he never carried a knife. They believe that Tracie Andrews took a knife out with her that night.

And what of the confession? She is doing it to save her own skin, they believe, because she knows that she has to admit her crime before she is considered for parole.

Another woman could offer no explanation as to her motives, and was desperate to find out why she killed... again, and again and again...

4

DEATH ROW INTERVIEW WITH RHONDA BELLE MARTIN

Allen Rankin

"I gave all the ones I done it to nice funerals"

FOR 17 years Rhonda Belle Martin kept a terrible secret while she added tombstone after tombstone to her family's burial plots in two cemeteries.

She was not much to look at — just a plain, middle-aged, bespectacled woman of the kind to be seen any day in any supermarket. But Rhonda Martin's shopping-lists often included arsenic. And one by one she murdered six people and paralysed a seventh.

Her victims, she said, were "the ones closest to me, the ones I loved the most." They comprised her mother, two of her five husbands and three of her little daughters.

All these murders went undetected until she married her stepson, a 30-year-old sailor, and began to give him the same "affection" — arsenic-laced ant poison.

Ronald Martin was admitted to hospital, paralysed from the waist down. Tests carried out to diagnose his mystery ailment found arsenic in his hair. The stepmother who had become his bride was arrested. She confessed to six slayings, and an attempted seventh.

On July 16th, 1956, she was convicted on the specimen

count of one of those murders and sentenced to be executed in the electric chair. And on October 3rd, 1957, I went to see her at her new address: Death Row, Jefferson County Jail, Alabama.

It was a calm and sombre Mrs. Martin who was brought into the interview room. A big woman — 12 stone — she looked at me sadly through her horn-rimmed glasses. And there was something about her eyes that seemed to give them a magnetic attraction.

I had wondered how such an ordinary-looking woman could have persuaded a stepson nearly 20 years her junior to become her fifth husband. Perhaps those eyes were the answer.

The jail matron who led her in said Mrs. Martin had been a model prisoner and had made many friends among both officials and inmates in the year she had waited on Death Row. She had spent much of her time praying, reading her Bible and making dresses for sister convicts who needed them. She'd been "like a mother" to some of the girls and had made a special point of always seeing they were dressed smartly when they went to chapel on Sundays.

"You're not going to make me look bad, like some of those other magazines have done, are you?" she asked me suspiciously.

"I'm going to give you a fair interview," I promised. "I'm going to write down exactly what you say."

"All right, then," said Rhonda, "if you'll tell it like it is, like I am. A lot of people, them that don't know me, think I'm bad and mean, I guess ... think I'm terrible!

"They think I meant to do all that I did, but I could not help doing it!"

Tears came suddenly running down her face. We both knew that she would probably never read my account, that by the time it appeared in print she might be long dead.

"Just tell them what I was really like," Mrs. Martin said quietly. "That the people who knew me best, especially my dead loved ones, knew I always meant to be kind."

Toying with a good-luck charm — a silver four-leaf clover bracelet one of the prison officials had given her — she proceeded to tell me what she was "really like" in her own eyes. This is how the interview went ...

Mrs. Martin, so I can get it straight to start with, will you tell me who the six people were you killed?

Yes. [Counting on her fingers.] My little Emogene, two and a half, was the first one. She was sweet, pretty as a picture, made friends with everybody. I couldn't have loved her more.

That was your daughter Emogene, who died suddenly in 1939, at your mother's house on Wolf Ridge Road near Mobile?

No. That's where I put the poison powder in her milk, but she died with convulsions in the Mobile hospital about two and a half hours later. I rushed her to the hospital and gave her the best of care. No one can ever say I didn't give all of them the very best of care!

And you killed the other five with liquid poison, ant poison?

Yes, there was George [Garret] ... He was the father of all my girls and the one I was happiest with. I put ant poison in his whisky — two or three teaspoonfuls, I reckon — and he died a little after Emogene.

George was a railwayman, and you were living in Montgomery, on May Street, at the time that happened?

Yes, that's where I had the happiest time in my life ... on May Street with my little girls, before all this started. Then there was Carolyn. She died at St. Margaret's Hospital in May, 1940.

After you put ant poison in her milk?

Yes, I had to give it to her two or three times. Carolyn was awfully smart and pretty as a picture. It was her first year in school, and her teacher was so proud of her ... he came and told me how bright she was. That, of course, was before Carolyn had to stop school, just a little before we had to bury her that May. She was six.

And the next?

That was Ellyn, eleven, in the fourth grade. But she was

sickly . . . had some kind of paralysis, before I give it to her. We had to bury her about three years after Carolyn. Then came Mama. I was living back with her on Wolf Ridge Road at the time, in 1944. I was devoted to Mama. I was living with her after my stepdaddy died so she'd have somebody to stay with her, wouldn't be herself. I was working at the paper mill, but Mama and I were together a lot. She loved flowers and raised them for the street-market, and I'd help her in the garden, and we'd take in sewing . . . Then it came over me again, and I gave the ant poison to Mama and she died.

Next?

Claude Martin.

He was your fourth husband? A foreman at the glass factory in Montgomery? The one who died suddenly in 1951 after you put ant poison in his coffee?

Yes.

How many times did you doctor his coffee?

Three or four different times.

Rhonda Belle, you were tried and given the death penalty for only one murder count — the murder of Claude Martin. The state charged you did it to collect his life insurance.

I didn't! I wouldn't have thought of doing such a terrible thing for insurance money! I could never have been so mean as that! I'm just not that kind of person!

Did you have any life insurance on Martin?

Yes, I had some with Metropolitan and he had some with Hazel-Atlas. How much I don't know, but neither of us had much.

Did he change these policies before he died?

Yes.

Did the money go to his son, Ronald?

No, it went to me. But it wasn't but very little . . . somewhere between three and four thousand, and part of it went to his youngest daughter to finish school on. They just don't understand. I didn't do it for that. I didn't want Claude to die. I didn't want anybody to die! If I'd gained a thing in the world from any of it but a whole lot of worry! I paid more for Claude's funeral than I got from the insurance. I gave him a nice funeral!

That was very thoughtful of you, Mrs. Martin.

Yes. And I was good to him before he died. I took him to the hospital and stayed with him every minute. I really care for him good. I'd help him get in and out of the car when he got so he couldn't even walk. But there was something wrong somewhere. I don't know *why* I didn't tell all those doctors what was really the matter with Claude.

You say you loved Claude Martin?

Yes, I loved and respected him. He was a good man. He didn't drink and he didn't smoke. And after I married him I never drank or smoked while he was alive. And I quit work at the glass factory so I could stay at home and be a mother to his three growing-up daughters. I didn't want to set a bad example before the girls ... to do anything around them I wouldn't have done before my own children They seemed to think a lot of me ... not as much as of their own mother, of course, but a lot.

I gave all the ones I done it to nice funerals and I went out and put flowers on the graves every week. And I'd go with Claude to put flowers on his first wife's grave.

I couldn't have been a better nurse to Claude after he got sick from the poison in his coffee. When he began hurting and moaning and would ask me to rub him I'd do it like I did for all the rest of 'em. And I'd get him a hot water bottle or anything he wanted.

After we buried Claude I even had his first wife dug up and laid beside him in a special plot. I though he'd like that, and I wanted it for him.

Rhonda Belle, how long after Claude died did you marry his son, Ronald?

About eight months, I think. When Bud's daddy — I called Ronald Bud — was on his death bed he asked Bud to see that I was well taken care of. I was nice to Bud, treated him like a mother, and it wasn't long before he asked me to marry him.

What did you say?

At first I told him I didn't think it was right ... that there was too much difference in our ages and he needed a young wife. But he said, no, he'd never seen a woman before that he wanted to marry and he'd have asked me to marry him even if his daddy hadn't asked him that. So I married him. He didn't seem to care much for people of his own age and we got along fine. We both like to fish. We bought a motor and a boat and I was a good wife to him in every way.

Mrs. Martin, was it Ronald Martin himself who first suspected you were poisoning him?

No, indeed it wasn't. Bud wouldn't have dreamed I would do such a thing. It was the doctors over at the Veterans' Hospital at Biloxi, and *I* was the cause of him going over there. The doctors in Mobile said they'd done all they could for him and they couldn't work out what was wrong with him. So I insisted that he go over to the Veteran's Hospital where he could get the best possible attention. I took the best possible care of Bud, visited him every day ... but he kept getting sicker, more and more paralysed.

That was because you had put ant poison in his drinks at your Mobile place?

Yes. I put it in his coffee several times the month before that ... Why didn't I tell the doctors what was the matter with him? That's what I want to know! Why didn't I tell them?

It was the doctors at the hospital who suggested a test be run on Ronald's hair, and they found it loaded with arsenic?

That's right.

Tell me about your arrest.

Well, I was working as a waitress. A man come in there and stayed nearly all day, just drinking coffee and watching me and not saying anything. I didn't know it, but he was Mr. Coley, a state investigator. When I got off at three he walked up and showed me his badge and said the chief of police wanted to talked to me.

Did you know why you were being arrested?

I didn't know, but I had a good idea. I'd been waiting for it to happen for a long time.

You denied everything for three or four days.

Yes, but after they took me to Montgomery and told me they'd dug up Claude and were going to dig up the rest I decided to tell them everything.

You poured out the whole story to Solicitor William F. Thetford, Detective T. T. Ward and State Investigator Willie B. Paiter. Why?

Seems like something suddenly came over me and I just had to let it all go. Nobody but my God knows what I went through holding it all back all these years, and what a relief it was to tell it!

You were interviewed by psychiatrists. What did they say?

Some of them asked me questions. But another one, he just come and started telling me things about myself. He had his mind made up before he come in — that's the way I feel about it. He told me I killed him [Claude Martin] so I could marry his son. That wasn't so, because Ronald was off in the navy then and I didn't know anything about him. He told me I killed people to get rid of responsibility, and I don't think that was so, either.

Mrs. Martin, how does your last husband, Ronald Martin, feel about you now?

The last letter I had from him he told me he loves me just as much as he ever did. That he was just sorry there wasn't something more that he could do to help me.

He was almost totally paralysed when they found his trouble. How is he doing now?

Bud's getting better, I hope and pray to God! The last letter I got from him he said he was walking without a stick now. But he said his hands weren't getting better as fast as his feet. He still can't hardly write yet.

Did your present husband have any insurance?

A little — about $3000, I think, at the paper mill.

Payable to you?

Yes

Were you in your mother's will?

Yes.

What did you get when she died?

One of her cars and one-fourth of her estate.

How much did that estate amount to?

Just $750. But anybody who thinks I could have *ever* killed *anybody* for insurance or something like that just doesn't know me! Them that do know me know I'm not a mean, bad person at all!

Rhonda Belle, it is well known that you have attracted many men in your life. Of your five husbands, the two you didn't poison were divorced by you. How do you personally account for the love and loyalty you have elicited from men?

I don't know I never asked them why. I guess it's because when I had a husband, I took care of his house and I took care of him. I never had one complaint about his meals or he never accused me of going out with another man. He always knew where he could find me — at home. I did always want a home of my own, and I never did get one ... only rented places. My husbands just never had any complaints of any kind, that's all.

Except one.

Yes, sir. Except one. That thing that would come over me about the poison was the one bad thing that was wrong with me ... the only really *bad* thing, though the Lord know I didn't ever claim to be perfect.

Tell me why you did it, Rhonda Belle ... why you poisoned them.

I wish you or somebody would tell *me* why! That's what I've never been able to understand! I never wanted to kill anybody! And I never thought about it once before I done it! If I'd thought about it beforehand I never would have done it!

But, since you did it the first time, haven't you had 17 years to think, to experience anxiety, to have nightmares?

Yes, but it seemed like I wouldn't think about the others — the ones in their graves — when I'd do it again. And the dreams I'd have about the ones that were gone weren't nightmares. They were always pleasant dreams ... dreams back with Mama or George or Claude or my little girls all alive.

Mrs. Martin, did you have a compulsion at these times, a feeling that you had to kill?

No! No! I tell you I never intended to kill anybody! I just wanted to love them, to nurse them, to take care of them! {Sobbing] I love them! I loved them all, don't you understand?

The ones I done it to the ones I was closest to, the ones I loved the best! Once they were sick I took the very best care of them I could. It would break my heart to see them suffer, to hear them cry out, "Mama, it hurts so! Please help me!"

Mrs. Martin, you are alive today because the governor has granted you a 14-day stay of execution in order that you might have a sanity hearing. Do you think you're crazy?

I just don't know ... don't know. I don't *seem* to be crazy ... I've always been able to work good and things life that. I swear to God I don't know *what* come over me to make me do it again and again. Ain't nobody but me and my God knows what doing it every time made me suffer inside. Wondering about why I did it worries me more than going to the electric chair.

There must be somebody who could tell me that, anyway, before I die. Some scientists or something! If they could, I'd undergo any kind of test, no matter what, just so they could tell me why I done all I did ... especially to my little children.

Mrs. Martin, one newspaper reporter has hinted that when your first child, Adelaide, died of pneumonia, something may have snapped in your brain. Can you tell me something about Adelaide?

There isn't much to tell ... except that I'd always wanted children and I was late in having any. When Adelaide finally came she was born afflicted. I loved her terribly. I sat over her and nursed her day and night for the three years and four months she lived. When she died it could have done something to me ... I don't know.

Do you think it's possible that after that you wanted others you love to be sick in bed where you could nurse them and care for them and have them all to yourself as you did with Adelaide?

I never thought of that. I don't know if it was that, or what it was.

Rhonda Belle, would you try to reconstruct the scene and the circumstances of your first poisoning?

Yes, I'll try. I was about thirty-seven then, or close to it, and George, my second husband, was still alive, and I was visiting Mama and my stepfather at the place on Wolf Ridge Road. I was sewing the children's clothes, getting them all fixed up to go back to Montgomery and to school.

But your daughter Emogene was too young to go to school ... just two and a half ... still toddling around the house. When did you first think of poisoning Emogene?

I didn't think of it at all. The idea of poison never did enter my head until my stepfather got to talking about it. He told us there was a corn crib out in the field. And he told us not to go near the crib or let the children near it, because he told us what was in there — some white powder, some cotton poison he used in the field. He told us not to go near it so much that that last day I went back and looked at it, and I picked some of it up.

And put it in Emogene's milk? Why, Mrs. Martin?

I wish someone could tell me. Something just come over me, and two hours after Emogene drank the milk she fell with a convulsion. We rushed her to the hospital and I told them, because she died so quick, I wondered if she hadn't got poisoned.

You told them that?

Yes, because the week before there was a dog died in the neighbourhood, poisoned. I told them I wondered if she hadn't got hold of some of that. That's why the coroner came in on it and they said they were going to make the tests for poisoning.

And they made those tests?

I don't know. I don't know why they didn't find out. They told me they were going to send Emogene's organs to Auburn [the state toxicology and crime investigation laboratory]. It was a month or more before we heard any more about it.

Did you worry in that month, Mrs. Martin? Worry for fear of being found out?

I was worried because Emogene was dead. Only my God knows how much I was worried. Then the coroner in Mobile decided there wasn't nothing wrong about the way Emogene died, and he signed a certificate, and they never asked us any more questions ...

Rhonda Belle, is it true you used the same bottle of ant poison on the last five?

No, I believe I used the first bottle three times. That must have been on George, Carolyn and Ellyn. Then, I believe, I lost that bottle ... I don't see why they had to have that man [a chemist] come up and say what he did in court — that I bought a bottle from him. I told them myself I bought the ant poison from him. I guess I've bought a number of bottles of it. When I was living with Claude we had a lot of ants, and I used some of it for that too. I never tried to hide the bottle. It was right there on the kitchen shelf for anyone to see. But it seemed like a lot of 'em were against me at the trial.

Did you have a horror of that poison bottle, a horror you might use it again?

No. In between times I just didn't ever think about it, except when I needed it for ants.

Mrs. Martin, they say you've been mighty nice to the other inmates here. That you've made a lot of friends in prison.

I hope so. I like to care for people, especially people in trouble. I'm able to keep busy at it here. I'm good at sewing ... fancy work and embroidery I try to keep the other girls' clothes up so they look nice. If any of 'em need altering, I do that. I made the draperies for the chapel, and I always see they got clothes fit to wear to church. They've been mighty good to me too. Everybody has, ever since they first arrested me. I was afraid at first. I thought maybe they'd beat me or something. But they've all been as nice and polite as they could be. Treated me like a lady.

Do you know the date that you're scheduled to . . .

Yes, if I don't get another stay I'll sit down in the electric chair on the eleventh, in eight days. They didn't tell me all the other times I was scheduled to die, because I've got a bad heart and have attacks. But I had some attacks anyway. They thought the suspense of not knowing was worse on me than telling me when. So they've told me.

If you don't get another reprieve, you'll have one last clemency hearing before the governor a week from today.

Yes, I've made myself a nice dress, black and white, to go to my hearing. I've always tried to look the best I possibly could. And I've made myself a new purse, black and white. And I'll wear these seashell earrings. A matron here gave them to me as a gift.

What will you tell the governor?

There's nothing I *can* tell him much. I just want to ask him to please commute my sentence to life. I don't want to get out, ever. If I was to get out I might do the same thing over again. I'm afraid I would. I wish they had caught me a long time ago and put me in here so I couldn't have done all I did. But I'm hoping they'll let me live. I like to care for people, and there'd be a lot I could do in here to help somebody else. I could be more of a use that way than just being dead.

Mrs. Martin, if your sentence is not commuted to life, are you prepared to die?

Well, you've never seen anybody who was ready to sit down in the electric chair. But if that's what it's got to be, that's what it will be. I've made my peace with God and I know He has forgiven me and a lot of others have forgiven me. I guess I've made more friends, got more letters, especially from Christian women, than at any time in my life before. Anything that happens now is for God to say. I'm ready for whichever way it turns. But, naturally, I hope they'll let me live and be of some use.

Is there anything else you'd like to say, Rhonda Belle?

No, I guess not. Except I hope them scientists who are so smart at everything else can find out why I done it all and tell me. I hope I'll know before I die. I'd give anything, go through anything, to know. And I hope people won't remember me as mean and bad ... like those that really knew me knew I never was ...

So ended the interview. As I shook hands with Rhonda Belle Martin and wished her well I wondered if she would still be alive to read this story when it was published.

Still gazing at her good-luck charm, the silver four leaf clover, this woman with the darkest, most tortured eyes I have ever seen walked away towards her still unknown fate. The last thing I heard her mutter was: "There must have been something wrong with me ... something wrong."

There was no reprieve. On the appointed day, October 11th, 1957, Rhonda Belle Martin walked to the chamber, clutching a New Testament. Behind her, in her cell, she left a note asking that her body be turned over to medical authorities because she wanted them "to find out why I committed the crimes I committed. I can't understand it, for I had no reason whatsoever. There's definitely something wrong ..."

At a few minutes after midnight she was strapped into the electric chair and asked if she had anything to say. She shook her head silently. The switch was thrown, electricity surged through her body, she stiffened and was duly pronounced dead.

Forty-one years later another frail old lady faced death in the electric chair with nothing to say ...

5

THE TROUBLE WITH JUDY

Sam Roen and A.W. Moss

"She was different from anybody... a super intelligent woman"

THERE WERE just too many coincidences in the life of Judy Buenoano. And most of them had been fatal for her nearest and dearest, or so it seemed to Detective Ted Chamberlain of Florida's Pensacola, police.

Sitting at the hospital bedside of a man lucky to be alive after his car was dynamited, Chamberlain had asked: "Who would benefit from your death?"

The answer was the man's girl friend Judy Buenoano, who had insured his life for $500,000 with herself as the beneficiary.

That made the investigator suspicious. He became even more inquisitive when the victim disclosed that a few months earlier he'd ended up in hospital after eating one of Judy's salads.

Probing further, Chamberlain discovered that the car-bomb casualty was by no means the first person to have had an unfortunate relationship with Judy Buenoano. At least three of those closest to her had died suddenly, and each time she had collected the insurance.

The chain of suspicious deaths had started 13 years earlier in 1971 when Judy's first husband, an air force sergeant named James Goodyear, suddenly fell ill, dying shortly afterwards in hospital in Orlando. To check out the circumstances of that death, Chamberlain picked up his phone and sought the help of B. B. "Dusty" Rhodes, an Orlando-based investigator for the Florida state attorney.

Intrigued by the Pensacola detective's brief outline of what lay behind his request, Rhodes sped off to the Bureau of Vital Statistics and searched out the date of death of James Edgar Goodyear, 37. The subject, a returned Vietnam veteran, had died in the US Naval Training Centre Hospital in Orlando on September 16th, 1971. He had been buried in the Chapel Hill Cemetery, just outside Orlando. His widow Judy was at that time 28.

By exploring records and talking to navy intelligence personnel, Rhodes learned that Goodyear's attending physician was Dr. Harley T. Cloistermann who had long since left the navy and now had a practice in Pittsburgh. When contacted, Cloisterman said that he did not remember the patient, or the signing of his death certificate in Orlando.

Consulting the hospital records concerning James Goodyear, the investigator read: "This 37-year-old, admitted with a two-week history of nausea, vomiting, diarrhoea and abnormal liver function tests ... This man returned from South Vietnam three months ago, following a one-year tour of duty. During that time he took his anti-malarials and was not ill while on that tour of duty. He returned to the United States in June, 1971, and since that time has not been feeling well, tending to tire easily, associated with decrease in appetite and increased abdominal distention."

Dr. Cloistermann's report also noted Mrs. Goodyear's comments and observations regarding her husband at the time of his malady: "A history related by his wife that he manifested some evidence of cerebral involvement with somewhat bizarre behaviour and mild disorientation." The doctor also wrote that the wife "stated that she thought his eye membranes were jaundiced."

Rhodes took the medical report to Dr. Thomas Hegert, the medical examiner for central Florida, explaining that foul play was suspected. It was known that Judy Buenoano's son Michael, from a previous relationship, had been exposed to arsenic poisoning which had caused him to become a quadraplegic. The boy's death, however, was not caused by arsenic but by drowning, in suspicious circumstances.

Hegert listened intently as Rhodes related the facts he had accumulated. Then Rhodes asked the doctor if Goodyear's death could be attributed to arsenic poisoning.

Hegert said that it was not inconsistent with arsenic poisoning.

With the information that awakened suspicion which had rested quietly for 12 years, Rhodes now went before his boss, State Attorney Robert Eagan, and attention turned to the possible exhumation of James Goodyear's body.

Dr. Hegert had indicated that there had been tissue samples taken at the autopsy of Goodyear, and that they "should still be in the custody of the military authorities."

Rhodes soon located them and they were sent to the Armed Forces Institute of Pathology in Washington, DC, for examination. The possible exhumation of Goodyear's body would hinge on the results.

While the investigation moved on in Orlando a parallel probe was being conducted in the town of Trinidad, Colorado, prompted by the suspicious death of Bobby Joe Morris, 35, successor to Goodyear as Judy Buenoano's partner, and also covered by an insurance policy that named her as the beneficiary.

Dusty Rhodes was never able to bring to light any legal proof of Judy's marriage to Morris. He described their relationship as "lovers — live-in, or whatever you want to call it."

Rhodes next interviewed a man who was the link between Judy and Bobby Joe. Chuck Dorsett confessed to the investigator that he'd had "a closeness with Judy back in 1970–71." They met when Chuck hired her for part-time work at the used-car agency he ran in Orlando.

Dusty asked him if they had met before her husband went to Vietnam and he replied: "That's correct." He also admitted that he had met Judy's husband "two or three times" when he came to the agency.

Some time after Goodyear went overseas Chuck moved to Pensacola. He said that Judy did not let their friendship die, and phoned him in Pensacola. He agreed to drive to Orlando to meet her. He said that they stayed in a motel near his old car agency. They had several such meetings over a period of several months.

"Up until her husband's return from Vietnam?" Rhodes inquired.

"That's correct."

Rhodes asked: "Just when did you hear from Judy again after her husband got back from Vietnam?"

Chuck said that he got a call from Judy two or three days before James Goodyear died, "asking me to come down ... that he was very ill." Chuck Dorsett duly went to Orlando, but Goodyear was dead before he arrived. Chuck told Rhodes: "She asked me to go to the funeral with her the next day." He said he did so, adding that he stayed with Judy in her home on the night of the funeral. She had converted one of her rooms into a bedroom which he used rather than hers. But, he said, "she later came in and got in bed with me."

Dusty asked: "Did she come to bed with you for the purpose of having sex with you?"

"I would imagine that would be perfectly normal."

Rhodes pursued: "Did it strike you as odd that the woman who had just buried her husband within the last 24 or 48 hours was acting like that?"

"I couldn't believe it ... I really couldn't believe it."

"So she was not a grieving widow?"

"Not that I could possibly see."

Dorsett said that he left Orlando after a day or two, then returned a couple of weeks later with Bobby Joe Morris.

Introductions were made and the group partied, had drinks, sent out for steaks and "lived it up."

He said that Judy and Bobby Joe lost no time in forming "a mutual admiration society. Bobby Joe Morris thought Judy Goodyear had money and Judy imagined that Bobby Joe had money — that Bobby Joe's family owned a utility company up there in Pensacola."

Rhodes gathered from Dorsett that Bobby Joe had taken over from him with Judy.

Turning to the death of James Goodyear, Rhodes asked what he had heard about it. Dorsett revealed that an old friend had told him: "You sure were lucky to get away from that broad" — meaning Judy Goodyear.

The friend had continued: "I'm sure she must have killed her husband . . . She came to me and asked me what kind of poison to use."

Dorsett said the friend was now dead, adding that two more acquaintances had made similar observations. "It seemed to be a joke that I was very lucky that I didn't get myself killed."

Continuing interrogation of Dorsett produced the disclosure that Judy had allegedly retained a hit-man to kill James Goodyear. Dorsett recalled that Judy had "paid an individual to go up to Orlando and shoot her husband . . . I think the price was $2,500." He explained that the plan was for the hit-man to call her — and that phone call would be her signal to tell her husband that the child-care centre she managed was being robbed. When James rushed to the centre he was to be shot.

Making further inquiries, Rhodes picked up the first name of a woman — Jan — who was said to have been a close friend of Judy's.

Traced to Delaware where she was interviewed, Jan said that she had met Judy in 1968 or 1969, had lived with her for a short time and went to work for her at the child-care centre. She also revealed that she had dated Bobby Joe Morris after Judy introduced them.

She gave a rundown on the personal life of the

Goodyears, stating that Judy was "sick and tired of being married to James." There were also some odd things about Judy's son Michael, and her relationship with the child. Jan said that Michael had seemed to give Judy problems, so she put him in a special school in Miami.

"I don't know if he was brain-damaged or something, but there was something wrong with him ... yeah." When Rhodes inquired whether Michael was retarded, Jan replied: "Maybe. Judy kept saying that he was a genius, but he could have been retarded or brain-damaged."

When Rhodes brought his questioning around to the subject of James Goodyear's death Jan revealed that she and Judy had both talked about poisoning their husbands. Jan proceeded with a divorce, but she listened in awe as Judy prescribed her cure for her marital problems — arsenic. Their conversations about getting rid of their husbands took place more than a year before James Goodyear's death. They had joked about killing their husbands by putting arsenic in their tomato juice, or macaroni salad.

Questioned about Goodyear's life insurance, Jan was not able to fix the beneficiary value, but thought that it was $10,000, or enough to pay off the mortgage on Judy's house.

Rhodes asked if Judy ever told her how much she got in insurance money. Jan told him: "Yeah. She said a couple of hundred thousand, but that could have meant $10,000. When you're dealing with Judy, you very often have to remove zeros."

"How did Judy spend the insurance pay-outs?"

"She bought a new Cadillac ... blue with a white top — beautiful car. I think she paid cash," said Jan, adding that Judy had also had a swimming pool installed at her home. "She bought a couple of cars and traded in cars twice at least ... She also bought me a car."

Jan went on to say that Judy's house in Orlando had been damaged in a fire — and there was a suspicion of arson. But apparently that was not established, because

Judy collected the insurance money.

Jan and Judy moved to Pensacola, where they lived together until Jan returned to Orlando. "After I left, I heard that Bobby Joe Morris bought her, or built her, a house ... I think that was in January, 1972." Jan stated that Judy and Bobby Joe had lived together after she (Jan) left Pensacola.

Rhodes then turned the questioning to Michael. Jan said that she thought Judy had insurance on her son, adding that Judy was "ashamed of him." Jan said that the reason for Judy's feelings about Michael was "because he was different. Judy was something of a perfectionist, everything had to be perfect ... and Michael wasn't."

Rhodes asked about Judy's occupation "other than the day care centre" and also if she'd ever worked as a nurse. Jan replied: "I think she worked as a nurse's aide, which led her to say that she was a registered nurse. She also told people that she was a lawyer, specialising in constitutional law."

Rhodes brought the questioning back to James, asking if Judy had ever told her the reason for James's death. Jan said: "She told me that when the guys over in Vietnam were innoculated against the black plague they got a bad viral, or something. A lot of people got sick from it and died of the black plague."

Jan added that Judy was "generous. She would give you the shirt off her back.

"She was a nice person ... do anything for you. She lied a lot — or embellished. Maybe that would be a kinder way to put it. She embellished everything."

Rhodes then met Leona Handy, who'd known Judy in September or October 1971, just about the time of James Goodyear's death.

Leona said: "She was a likeable person. She was different from anybody I'd ever been around, a super-intelligent woman ... always telling me things that she had done, and it was just fascinating to be around her. Judy had a lot of money. She told me that she had got it from selling real estate."

Leona added that Judy told her that she had received, or was about to receive, $40,000 for her house that had burned. She paused, then revealed: "Judy said she burned her house to collect insurance on it."

Rhodes asked if Leona knew anything about the death of James Goodyear and she said: "She told me at that time that he died from a bug that he had picked up in Vietnam."

Leona went on to say that she and her husband were having marital problems at this time and Judy visited her. "It was on a Saturday and she started telling me how I could kill my husband, because *she* had killed *her* husband and she knew that I would not get caught at it."

Leona said that she and Judy went to a local grocery store, where they talked about their problems. "She was walking down the aisles with me and she started telling me how I could get some poison. She said it was a fly-bait poison that had a lot of arsenic in it. I think she told me that I could give it to him in some milk and nobody would ever know it."

Leona then looked directly at Rhodes and stated: "She said the reason she knew that nobody would ever know it was because she killed her husband with the same stuff." Leona said she reminded Judy that she had explained James's death as the result of something he'd picked up in Vietnam, and Judy then confessed to her that she had told everybody that, but that she "really did kill him."

Rhodes asked if Judy told her why she'd killed James.

"For his money ... for insurance," Leona replied, saying that Judy claimed that she "got several hundred thousand dollars from killing her husband."

Leona was not sure how Judy had administered the arsenic. But she added: "I'm almost positive that she gave it to him in his milk, because he liked milk."

Leona agreed that Judy's stories might well be long on fantasy and short on truth. But she emphasised: "The trouble was I did believe her when she told me how she killed her husband — because she was as serious as a heart attack about wanting to help me kill mine."

Leona said she did not report what Judy had told her about James Goodyear's death because she was afraid of her. "Judy wanted me to think that she was into the Mafia. She wanted me to think that she had a lot of backing of people in the underworld."

The witness added that later that same day she'd revealed to her husband the story that she had been told in confidence. She recalled: "She was so serious that I went straight to him and told him what Judy had told me about killing.

"I said, 'Paul, don't you drink anything or eat anything that that woman prepares for you, because she is real, real serious.'"

On February 17th, 1984, Dr. Jerry Spencer of the Armed Forces Institute of Pathology in Washington, DC, contacted Rhodes and revealed that the examination of James Goodyear's tissue samples had disclosed the presence of arsenic.

Meanwhile Bobby Joe Morris's body had been exhumed in Colorado, and the cause of his death had been found to be arsenic poisoning.

Applying for the exhumation of James Goodyear, State Attorney Eagan cited evidence which included the fact that Judy Buenoano had been the beneficiary of Morris's $30,000 life insurance policy.

Eagan also noted: "On May 13th, 1980, Michael, the 19-year-old son of Judy Goodyear (Buenoano) drowned in Santa Rosa County, Florida, while on a fishing trip with his mother, as a result of the capsizing of a canoe that they occupied ... an autopsy revealed large amounts of arsenic in his system. Approximately $125,000 insurance on his life was paid to Judy Goodyear."

The requested exhumation order was issued.

Meanwhile in Pensacola Ted Chamberlain was still immersed in the mysteries of the deaths of Michael Goodyear and Bobby Joe Morris. The investigation of

Michael's drowning tied in with the suspicions regarding Bobby Joe's death on January 26th, 1978, in Colorado and was further linked to the miraculous escape from death of Judy Buenoano's boy friend John Gentry whose car exploded in Pensacola on June 25th, 1983.

In the circumstances of Michael's drowning, the official report stated: "At the time of the 'accident,' Michael Goodyear was wearing full leg-braces and a device on his right arm which operated a prosthetic hand, through cables and braces with the muscles of his shoulder." His doctor stated that Michael "was completely immobile, knees down and elbows down. He could not walk, even with the braces — and he had no control with his arms. It would be quite impossible for the boy to swim."

The report also stated that there was "reason to doubt the credibility of his mother's statements." Due to the slow current of the river, "it would be most difficult to tip the canoe over by striking a submerged object" (as claimed by Judy).

The report concluded that Michael's "decision to go canoeing in his physical condition may evidence a reckless disregard of the possible consequences. But his mother's decision to put him in that canoe with only a ski-belt may be considered neglectful, if not bordering on criminal neglect."

Since then Judy had talked her latest lover, John Gentry, into signing up for a life insurance policy of half a million dollars, naming her as the beneficiary. And that was her fatal mistake, because this was a victim who lived to testify against her.

On the night of June 25th, 1983, Gentry's car blew up when he switched on the ignition to which dynamite had been wired. He later told Chamberlain that he had been taking capsules fed to him by Judy Buenoano. The capsules made him sick, and he ultimately stopped taking them. He gave the remaining pills to Chamberlain, who sent them to the FBI lab to be analysed.

When they came back with the information that they

were paraformaldehyde, Chamberlain went to the state attorney and tried to persuade him that Judy had been poisoning Gentry. But the state attorney told him that he needed more evidence to build a stronger case.

Meanwhile the authorities in Santa Rosa County, Florida, arrested Judy and brought her to trial for the murder of her son Michael.

The court heard that Judy had been embarrassed by this less than perfect boy who drooled, had a low IQ and wet his bed until he was a teenager. She was so ashamed of him that when he came home from Miami on his school holidays she got her friend Jan to drive him around at night so that he wouldn't be seen by her boy friends. During the day he sought the company of neighbours because his mother seldom spoke to him.

Joining the army on leaving school, he returned home on 10 days' leave, but shortly after rejoining his unit he reported sick. Numbness in his fingers and toes, diarrhoea and nausea were among his symptoms, and the doctors' diagnosis was lead poisoning. He said he had felt ill while he was still at home. As his condition deteriorated he became paralysed.

Discharged from the army, he was fitted with devices in an effort to enable him to walk and to pick up things by using a hook. Then on May 12th, 1980, he was sent home. The next day his mother took him fishing, sitting him on a chair in the middle of their canoe, without a life-jacket.

The canoe capsized and Michael drowned while Judy swam to safety. She rejected another angler's offer to search for Michael, saying, "No. It's too late — he's dead." A search was nevertheless made while she drank a beer. At first she said that the canoe had been overturned by her efforts to get rid of a snake which had got into the boat, but she later changed her story, claiming that the craft had capsized after striking a submerged log.

It was later discovered that while Michael was in hospital in the autumn of 1979 his signature had been forged on five life insurance policies which named his mother as beneficiary. The scam had brought Judy $108,000.

Convicted of Michael's first-degree murder on June 6th, 1984, the Black Widow — as she had become known — was sentenced to life in prison, with no hope of parole for 25 years. There was an additional term of 15 years to run concurrently for grand theft. This related to the insurance pay-out she had received as the beneficiary of Michael's policies.

On June 28th, 1984, James Goodyear's exhumed body was found to contain more than 10 times the lethal dose of arsenic, and on August 31st, 1984, a grand jury indicted Judy Buenoano for his first-degree murder.

A few days later the Black Widow — by now an infamous national figure — was whisked back to Pensacola, where she was tried for the attempted murder, by bombing, of her 38-year-old lover John Gentry.

Prosecutor Michael Patterson told the jurors that the bombing was "a cunning, cold, calculated and cruel attempt to collect an easy half a million dollars."

"I was in love with Judy, no doubt about it," Gentry told the jury. "I thought she was an extremely feminine lady. I thought she was very sweet and kind." She had taken him on a cruise to the Caribbean, for which she paid. But she had also taken out that hefty insurance policy on his life.

Attending a party with Gentry, after the meal Judy had said she wanted to spend the rest of the evening with her women friends and told him to go home. He left the restaurant, got into his car, switched on the ignition and was blasted by an explosion which embedded parts of the seat in his stomach, ripping away some of his liver and intestines and hurling glass through the windows of passing vehicles. He managed to stagger from his wrecked car. Then he collapsed.

The court heard that Detective Chamberlain had subsequently traced 33 phone calls made from Judy's house to a man friend in Alabama who purchased dynamite eight days before the car-bombing. Six days later the Alabama friend had been visited by Judy's 18-year-old son James. And the day before Gentry's car exploded he had purchased two car-speakers, leaving it to young James to install them for him . . .

Convicted of masterminding the murder attempt, Judy Buenoano was on November 6th, 1984, sentenced to 12 years in prison.

Her trial for the murder of James Goodyear began on October 21st, 1985, prosecutor Belvin Perry describing how she had told her friend Leona Handy that she could buy arsenic "in any supermarket."

Dusty Rhodes revealed that he had spent two years investigating the Black Widow, telling the jury of one incriminating discovery after another. And the defendant's friend Jan recalled how Judy had "joked" about killing their respective husbands with arsenic.

Judy's defence lawyers suggested that her husband could have contracted arsenic poisoning from a defoliant while serving in Vietnam, but a prosecution medical expert said that Goodyear would have had to have drunk 12 gallons of the defoliant to reach the level of arsenic found in his liver.

The court also heard that Goodyear's death had brought his widow $28,000 in life insurance and $64,000 in veteran's benefits. On November 26th, 1985, Judge Emerson Thompson sentenced Judy Buenoano to die in the electric chair.

"I didn't ever kill anybody!" she sobbed, and she continued to protest her innocence throughout the ensuing 13 years she was to spend on Death Row, where she crocheted and knitted babywear for sale by her daughter.

Finally, the appeals process having been exhausted, on Monday, March 30th, 1998, Judy Buenoano became the first woman to be executed in Florida for 150 years. Previously the last woman put to death in the state was a freed slave hanged in 1848 for slaying her former master.

Just before Judy Buenoano's execution John Gentry said: "If they would allow me, I would pull the switch myself. There are people so evil that they really don't need to be among a civilised society. She preyed on people who loved her."

His sentiments were apparently shared by the public, for there was very little outcry against her execution, as had been the case the previous month when Karla Faye Tucker was put to death by lethal injection in Texas.

Now a frail, bespectacled 54-year-old grandmother, the Black Widow chose a salad of broccoli, tomato and asparagus, with strawberries and a cup of tea as her last meal. Then prison guards helped her into "Old Sparky," Florida's 75-year-old electric chair back in use again following an overhaul after it malfunctioned in 1997 and a prisoner's head caught fire during his execution.

Asked if she wished to make a final statement, Judy Buenoano said, "No, sir." Then the current was switched on and one of the male witnesses fainted as her body arched in response to three massive power surges. Although smoke rose from her right leg during her 38-second electrocution, a post-mortem examination found that her death was instantaneous ... unlike those of the victims she poisoned.

6

CASTRATED WITH SCISSORS

Ed Browning

"The cost of providing him with the sex he demanded seemed to get more and more exorbitant"

TO SOME women, the ladies' man is an irresistible figure. To others he is a repulsive one. To still other women he is both irresistible and repulsive. Such split feelings are hard to resolve sometimes. To caress him or to kill him — which will it be?

Rick Williams inspired such feelings in women. This 13 stone, six-foot hunk went through women like Kleenex tissues: Use once and throw away.

Strangely, almost miraculously, Rick persuaded a woman to marry him despite his wandering eyes and cheating ways. Love was truly blind in her case: Blind to his habit of ogling other women, blind to the women who returned his gaze and welcomed him into their beds.

Optimistically, she began sharing the bed with him in his second-floor apartment on South Cornell Avenue, near Chicago's affluent Hyde Park area, hoping that she could reform his wayward ways.

Predictably, the marriage went downhill fast, though in truth, it wasn't a terribly long descent. In January, 1986, she decided she'd had enough and she walked out the door.

But there was a problem. She still felt strongly for Rick; she still loved him in spite of everything. She knew better, but she just couldn't help herself. And Williams, too, still felt attached to his wife. And so it was that they continued to maintain contact by telephone.

On March 13th, 1986, Williams' wife turned up at the Prairie Avenue district police station worried sick. She explained to the desk officer that she had tried to call her husband several times the previous afternoon about a matter of personal urgency.

She'd tried both his home and place of work, a company selling cemetery plots, but he was nowhere to be found. The reply from one of Williams' work colleagues even sounded ominous: Williams had not shown up at his job for the last two days and had not called to explain his absence.

So Williams' wife had gone to his apartment that night hoping to find him, but, as she explained to the police, her knocking was to no avail. No one answered the door.

Consequently, an officer made a routine call to the cemetery where Williams sold plots and confirmed the missing man's absence. Urged on by the wife's worried pleading, the desk officer told a uniformed officer to accompany her back to her husband's apartment.

The officer and the woman explained the reason for their visit to the building superintendent, who agreed to unlock Williams' door.

They found Williams inside. Dead. Three pairs of eyes immediately became fixed on the dead man's naked groin. His trousers and pants had been rolled down to intentionally expose the crude mutilation of his genitals.

The police officer ordered the other two outside while he secured the scene. He was not able to stay inside the apartment long himself: The corpse had evidently lain on the living-room floor for some time, and with the windows closed for winter, the odour of death was unbearable.

Detectives arrived in answer to the police officer's alert

and steeling themselves against both the sight and smell of the crime, began their work.

The victim had bled profusely, not only from the mutilation of his sex organs, but also from several gunshot wounds to the upper body. The whole area around his body, in fact, was blood-red.

Nearby, the sleuths found what appeared to be clues and possibly a motive for the murder: Small bags of white powder that looked like cocaine, a pair of scissors and a bloodstained steak knife.

Detectives noted that the apartment doors and windows were all properly secured. This could only mean that the victim knew his killer.

The little bags of white powder on the floor suggested a drug motive, but the method of murder implied something else. Castration of a victim usually meant a strong sexual motive.

Experience told sleuths that the first person to suspect in a murder is the victim's spouse. They knew that Williams' wife had first brought the matter of his absence to police, a not so unusual tactic among criminals trying to deflect suspicion. The wife had also admitted still being in love with Williams, although his philandering had made her an unhappy lady.

The philandering, in fact, was the fly in the ointment. Investigators did not even have to question Williams' wife to learn of his insatiable appetite for women. The proof was right before their eyes — on the walls surrounding the dead man's body.

Dozens of photographs of pretty women hung on the walls, silent witnesses to the grisly fate their common lover had suffered.

All the photos had apparently been taken by Williams himself. Some of the girls were shown standing next to him, smiling. Sleuths counted more then 100 shots all told — a very respectable number even for the most boastful Casanova.

More evidence of his success with the ladies was found

in a drawer following a more extensive search of the apartment. Rolls of film, when developed, showed that Williams liked to take photos of naked women in provocative poses.

In true Casanova style, he kept the rolls of film carefully labelled with the names of each subject, and judging by the models' carefree poses, they had stood before Williams' camera quite willingly.

But could one of the models have harboured enough resentment to have taken a knife or scissors to the macho cameraman where he most felt it? Lawmen made no move to arrest the murdered man's estranged wife, but they kept the option open until more evidence pointed to a stronger suspect in the case.

Whoever the killer was, he or she had had enough cool to pause after grisly mutilation and wash the blood off his or her hands: The kitchen sink was heavily stained with dried blood.

The body was removed for autopsy while detectives began their legwork, questioning other residents of the building. They didn't have much to say about their neighbour, only that he didn't seem to stay too long with any one girl. No surprise.

A check of Richard Williams' record at police head-quarters revealed more about the victim's background: Williams, it turned out, was a familiar figure. As a young man in the army, he'd raped and sodomised a woman he met in a bar, mistreating her for half a day before finally realeasing her.

Court-martialled, he received what he deserved — 35 years in Fort Leavenworth Prison. Williams cooled his ardour behind bars for six years before finally getting parole in 1965. For the next few years, he skittled through life and a long succession of women who briefly put up with his brutish ways before their sense of self-preservation finally took over. In 1971, one of them struck back, filing rape charges in Cook County court.

A backlog of cases delayed his trial for years; it wasn't

until four years later that Williams had his day in court — and another long prison term for sexual assault.

This time his cell was at Stateville Penitentiary and his stay was from seven to 21 years. His first bid for parole was denied, but in 1983, the parole board looked at Williams anew and decided he was a good bet to re-enter society.

A twice-convicted felon, Williams used his gift of persuasive gab to land a job at the cemetery, selling grave plots. He also did a little selling on the side — moonlighting in cocaine.

The results of the autopsy on Williams' corpse tended to discount a drug connection as a motive for one good reason. According to the medical examiner, Dr. Robert Stine, Williams had still been alive and breathing when his murderer cut off his testicles.

The lacerations showed unmistakably that scissors had been the instrument used. Williams, of course, had tried to defend himself; the deep cut on his left hand being visible proof of his unsuccessful efforts to ward off the scissors' blades.

A big man, Williams had apparently first been cut down to size by a couple of .22-calibre bullets to his chest. That was followed by several stabs to the body with the scissors. The castration followed. As Williams drew his last breath, he was still conscious of his ultimate humiliation.

The sexual mutilation spoke more of revenge than of murder over a drug deal. There was, of course, a slim possibility that the motive had both ingredients — sex and drugs.

Sleuths had plenty to speculate about, but no direction to follow as yet. The murder was already two days old — and the killer's trail was as cold as the Chicago snow outside.

Detectives did their best to put names to the nudes in Williams' photographic gallery. The rolls of films were marked only with the women's first names, which provided tantalising bait, but not much to sink a hook into.

A personal phone directory found in a drawer in the

dead man's apartment raised hopes of a quick solution to the problem, but a glance in it showed that Williams had been no more thorough in making his entries there than on his rolls of film. Each phone number had only a single name opposite. Evidently last names didn't exist in the vocabulary of the ladies' man.

Questioning Williams' former wife convinced sleuths that she was not a serious suspect in the case. All of her movements during the days before the murder could be accounted for. If the killer had indeed been a woman — and detectives were beginning to think more and more that way — then it was not the victim's ex-wife.

In fact, she proved helpful to the lawmen, providing names of Williams' friends. Two lawmen assigned to the case, Detectives Ed Schmidt and James Cassidy, went around to interview two of the acquaintances; and both had chapters to add to the plot.

The first revealed that Williams acted like a big-time photographer whenever he met a woman he wanted to bed down. Williams, he said, gave the girls a line about helping them out with their modelling careers, and most of them swallowed it.

Then it was just a question of leading them to his "studio," where it wasn't long before he got them out of their clothes and posing for the camera.

One of Williams' latest conquests was a woman introduced to him by his friend a month earlier. The friend said the woman, Jackie Foggie, had been tall and willowy, with an attractive face. With that combination, she'd naturally wanted to make money before the camera and agreed to Richard Williams' offer.

Not long after making the introductions, the friend saw Williams and Foggie leaving his studio together, apparently heading for Williams' apartment.

Sleuths didn't put too much stock in the story until the name Jackie Foggie came up again during an interview with another of Williams' friends. This time the friend said that on the night of March 13th — the day of the murder

— he had spoken to Williams over the phone.

Williams, he said, sounded very peeved, and continually broke off the conversation to shout at someone in the room with him.

At one point the friend heard the name "Jackie," then a woman's voice shouting in the background. The friend could also make out a TV set blaring, making his conversation with Williams even more difficult.

Asked whether he could recall the reason for the commotion, the friend replied that he'd heard the word "photographs" which led him to assume there was some dispute over photos that Williams had taken of the girl.

Williams, his friend well knew, was not the most tactful fellow when dealing with women. The thought crossed his mind that Williams could easily harm the complaining girl. But somehow the tables were turned and Williams ended up the victim. So was Jackie his killer?

Checking again through Williams' personal telephone directory, the two detectives came across a number for the woman in question. A call to the number got no answer, so the sleuths traced the address and drove over to talk to Jackie Foggie.

However, no one answered the door. The detectives located the building superintendent and she filled them in on her tenant's whereabuts.

Foggie, she told them, moved out without warning the previous day. The woman hadn't even had the courtesy to say she was going, and it was her boy friend who finally admitted that she had left.

The two detectives asked where her boy friend lived and were told he lived in the same building as Foggie. Soon they were standing before him and he told the officers Jackie left the day before without much ado.

He had asked her the reason for her abrupt move, but she'd just waved him off, saying she was tired of her apartment and wanted a change. And nothing he said would dissuade her.

"She's now got a place on Normal Avenue, not too far

from here," the young man volunteered.

At the suspect's new address, the officers knew they were on to something the moment Jackie Foggie opened the door: Her face had fresh scratches; long and deep — the kind made by someone fighting for his life. Consequently, the two lawmen calmly asked the woman to accompany them to headquarters.

For the next several hours the suspect was repeatedly asked to explain how she received the injuries to her face and why she had abruptly packed her bags and moved to another residence.

Each answer was lamer than the last. The crunch came, however, when she was told that a witness had heard her in the background while talking to the victim on the night of the murder.

As the sun of a new day broke over the horizon, the suspect leaned back in her chair and nodded acquiescence. She was ready to tell her story.

She had not known Williams for very long, a little more than a month, and a friend had introduced her. Williams flattered her about her figure and looks and suggested that he could do a lot for her career in modelling.

Some nude photographic sessions followed. Sexual sessions as well. Williams, she learned, was a forceful man who liked his sex varied and not always in traditional ways. Once, she said, he went too far, but she put up with it out of fear.

She still had high hopes of becoming a model, but as time went by and Williams failed to deliver on his promises, the cost of providing him with the sex he demanded seemed to get more and more exorbitant.

Williams, meanwhile, kept her docile with doses of drugs, specifically cocaine. He was starting to make big money with the stuff, buying jewellery and a new car. She, on the other hand, was getting hooked on coke. After a while, she wouldn't do without it — or without her easy supplier, Williams.

She began helping him prepare the little bags that

Williams sold to customers. In fact, the two of them were doing so on the night he died. They were also getting high on the drug and drinking alcohol, and by nightfall both were a mental and physical mess.

Foggie said she turned on the TV and began watching a show while Williams went in the other room to make a phone call. She was angry with him for forcing her to perform sex acts that she didn't like and for failing to come through on his promises to make her a model. She began shouting at him and he shouted back (the phone still in his hand).

Then he hung up the phone and picked up a .22-calibre revolver he kept in a drawer, brandishing the weapon in her direction. Foggie said she grabbed a can of hair spray and let Williams have the spray in the eyes.

Williams clutched his face and his gun fell to the floor. He tried to grab hold of her, scratching her face in the process. Foggie said she grabbed the gun and began squeezing the trigger time after time.

As Williams jerked back once, twice, three times, one arm still rubbed his eyes while the other flailed in search of her.

Williams finally fell to the floor, moaning. The revolver was empty. Of its five bullets two missed their mark and went into the walls. But Jackie wasn't finished yet.

Deliberately, she picked up the scissors which they'd been using to bag the cocaine. As Williams lay breathing heavily on the floor, she raised the scissors high over her head and brought the blades down squarely into his chest twice.

Then she took her final revenge. Unzipping his trousers, Jackie said she pulled them down to his ankles, then pulled down his underpants. A few moments later, Richard Williams was no longer a man.

As blood flowed around her ankles, she searched Williams' trouser pockets for his wallet; removing the cash. She also jerked a diamond ring off his finger and took the keys to his car. All that remained, she believed, was to wash the blood off her hands.

Jackie Foggie said she drove Williams' car back to her apartment, where she snorted some cocaine to give her courage. After a few hours' rest, she began thinking more calmly about what she'd done, realising that telltale evidence had to be destroyed.

Williams' car was a dead giveaway, so she drove it to a remote spot, doused it with petrol and added yet another burned-out derelict to Chicago's collection of abandoned vehicles.

Jackie Foggie was arraigned on murder charges on March 17th, 1986. The 19-year-old was ordered held without bond.

With the evidence gathered by detectives, the testimony of witnesses and the gruesome confession provided by Jackie herself, it looked like a sure thing for Assistant State Attorney George Velecich.

Nonetheless, with the backlog of cases facing the city courts, it was two years before the accused got to face her accusers. It was an uneven confrontation. Jackie knew she stood a good chance of life in prison for murder, mutilation, theft and destruction of property.

On the sound advice of her lawyer, Jackie proposed an outcome that would save taxpayers money and take into account the extenuating circumstances of her crime.

She agreed to plead guilty to involuntary manslaughter, sparing her the possibility of a long prison term for murder. Prosecutor Velecich felt it was a just deal, since the victim had been on record as a man of violence and who could easily have provoked an assault.

Therefore, on April 29th, 1988, Judge Christy Berkos sentenced Jackie Foggie to 15 years in the state prison.

7

BREAKING POINT

Brian Marriner

"I wasn't in a temper. She just had to die!"

They were an unlikely pair to form a friendship. Had they never met, one would not have become a killer. The other would be alive today.

At 28 Maria Hnatiuk, daughter of a Ukrainian father and a German mother, was a woman of the world, sophisticated, sexually experienced, and with a voracious erotic appetite. She had made love with men and women alike, but could never find the satisfaction she sought. The sexual urge was for her a permanent, insatiable itch.

She was also highly neurotic, with enhanced expectations from life — and in her delusions of grandeur she had had help along the way. Others helped make her feel "special"...

Rachael Lean was 18 and lived with her father in the village of Buxton, 10 miles north of Norwich. Every day she made her way to the RAF base at Coltishall, in Norfolk, where her father worked as a chief technician servicing Jaguar jet fighters. Rachael used the gym at the RAF base for her punishing schedule of circuit training and aerobics. She was keen to keep fit, and as she was due to start her first academic term at Southampton University within a few weeks she feared that she might not have the time or facilities there to keep in trim.

The villagers were used to seeing her cycling past on her way to the RAF base, and they were fond of her. She was one of them, a pleasant girl and a hope for the future. But then one day in late July 1995 she met Maria Hnatiuk, who shared her passion for aerobics, and Rachael introduced her to the RAF gym where they trained together and became friends.

Rachael didn't see the disturbed side of Maria's personality — until it was too late. All she knew was that Maria had moved into the neighbouring village with a boy friend and planned to launch a company with him to make their fortunes. The business was set up to sell swimwear, specialising in costumes modelled on those in the Baywatch TV series. Maria boasted to Rachael that she was going to become a director and have a company car. Rachael, flattered by the attentions of the older woman, was impressed by Maria's bragging.

There was a strong element of fantasy in all this, although the company had indeed been formed. It costs very little to register a new company, but considerably more to start making profits. And Maria was too unstable to be successful at anything which demanded diligence and sheer hard work.

She had grown up in Bristol but had left home at 18. She had considered becoming a teacher, but left college and worked for a bank and then an insurance company before moving to London in her early twenties to pursue a career with a music publicity company, which would bring her into contact with disc jockeys, agents and even pop stars. It was perhaps at this time that she began to think that some of the spurious glamour of the business might rub off on her. If she couldn't become a pop star herself, she might sleep with one...

She was later to have a six-month sexual relationship with a well-known disc jockey who took her on a pop-promotions tour abroad, and she developed high hopes of fame and fortune for herself. But long before that she had begun experimenting sexually and had a series of relationships. She had moved to Norwich in 1991, and after one relationship ended she attempted to burn down the lover's cottage. That was the first real indication of her unstable nature.

If the vagaries of fate are sometimes unfortunate, in this case they were downright malicious. Maria was to meet another man, and just as she had attempted to manipulate men for her own purposes — even if it meant breaking up marriages — she now met her match in a lover who manipulated her like a puppet.

Maria was working at a sports shop in Norwich in November 1991 when she met him at aerobics classes. It was a fateful meeting, destined to change several lives. He was married, but he began an affair with Maria, and in due course his wife confronted him about it. Because she was still very much in love with him and hoped to save her marriage, she suggested that he went away on his own for a few days to sort out his feelings. He said he would spend the weekend at a hotel and mull everything over — alone.

But his wife was later to say: "On the Monday he told me he had taken her to the hotel with him. I was devastated. We had two young children who adored him, and here he was risking throwing it all away for a bit on the side."

She decided to go to her husband's office to talk things over. She explained: "I didn't go there looking for a fight. I just wanted to see where we stood. But the first person I saw when I walked through the door was Maria. I just saw red. I grabbed her by her long blonde hair and pulled her off her chair to the floor. Then I coolly walked out."

She was lucky. She had floored the woman who stole her husband, but that rival was quite capable of murder, as she was later to prove. And Maria was the type of woman who once she had her claws in a man wouldn't let go easily. But she had picked the wrong man this time.

Maria became infatuated with him, allowing him to take

her over and change her completely. She had previously been very fashion-conscious, but now he made her wear dowdy clothes. At the home they set up together he made her wear PVC fetish outfits and dog collars. He hacked off her long blonde hair and refused to let her wear make-up. He was proving to be very dominant when he had a weaker partner in his power.

Now he was free to indulge his sexual fantasies. He forced Maria to make explicit calls to lesbian phone lines while he listened in, and he would sometimes beat her if the language was not sexy enough. Later he bullied her into bringing women home so that he could watch lesbian sex sessions before joining in. And throughout all this Maria had to shun contact with other men.

It may be hard for normal women to understand the spell this lover cast over Maria. She would do anything he asked. When he demanded details of her previous affairs she gave them — and that made him jealous and violent. A pop song on the radio would be enough to send him into a rage because it reminded him of Maria's past. It was later claimed that he made Maria prove her love for him by setting fire to the cottage of her previous lover. She poured petrol through the letterbox in the middle of the night and set it ablaze. The victim later said: "If the smoke hadn't woken me I'd be dead."

Over the course of four years, it was to be claimed, Maria's boy friend had transformed her from a normal woman into someone who would do his every bidding. He was described as a Svengali-type figure who dominated his mistress.

Typical of the sex games being played at this time was the correspondence between Maria and a model who in March 1995 had spotted a lonely hearts ad placed by Maria in her local newspaper. The model replied to the ad, and over the next three months Maria sent her pictures of herself in a skimpy black PVC body suit and black thigh-length boots. In return the model sent her some of her modelling pictures and a video.

Maria wrote back: "After seeing your fantastic face and body in the video, I've been fantasising a lot about you. I really want to drive you crazy and give you lots of pleasure. I can't wait to caress you, lick your body..."

Referring to her boy friend, she went on: "I love being the dominatrix, taking control. It brings him to his knees — I know I can bring you to yours. I have a male slave and I want you to be my female slave."

Their twice-weekly phone calls became increasingly steamy, until a meeting was arranged and the bisexual model went to visit Maria and her slave at their cottage. She was expecting a weekend of sexy fun, but she was left trembling in terror as the perverted Maria and her boy friend tried to lure her into kinky sex games. The model had insisted that she didn't want the man to be present, but after Maria had attempted to persuade her to be handcuffed she spotted him peering in through a window.

Significantly, when the two women first met at the railway station that night Maria had been glamorous and confident. By the next morning she was a different person, without make-up, wearing dowdy clothes and with her hair flattened. The model was to recall: "She was flitting about nervously. She seemed terrified of her man."

The question of just who was the dominant partner in the relationship between Maria and her boy friend was later to be determined by a jury. It seems that at this time Maria was in a downward mental spiral, as she was when she met Rachael Lean, who befriended her and was willing to give her moral support. It was Rachael's nature to be kind to people.

To punish Maria for spending a day with Rachael, her boy friend threw her out of his cottage and fixed her up with bed and breakfast accommodation right next to Rachael's home. Whether there was any sinister motive in choosing this accommodation remains unclear.

For a week Maria lived rough in what she described as the lowest point in her life, but she also said that she had to report to her boy friend every day, either in person or by prearranged phone calls.

On September 5th, 1995, she phoned Rachael in some distress and asked to meet. Rachael was perhaps naive, but she had other things on her mind, especially her forthcoming move to Southampton University. Nevertheless, she made time to see a friend in trouble. She was that sort of person.

The two met at the Naafi shop at the base and went for a 12-minute stroll down a dead-end country lane nearby. Just what happened next was known only to two people, and one of them is dead. But we know from the evidence that Maria produced a knife and stabbed the unsuspecting Rachael 57 times. The victim, fighting to protect herself, bled to death calling out Maria's name.

Her body was hidden in a nearby copse. Although she was reported missing that day, and her father flew home from Italy — where he was servicing jets for the Bosnian peace-keeping force — to join the search, Rachael lay undiscovered for five days. When she was found police felt it was significant that her leggings had been pulled down to expose her buttocks.

She had last been seen with Maria Hnatiuk, who was traced to Bristol where she was questioned for more than 50 hours but refused to admit her guilt. It was only months later when she realised the strength of the evidence against her that she confessed to her legal team. And even then she did not accept the full blame for her crime. She claimed that her boy friend's dominance made her feel that she had to kill Rachael in order to keep him.

It was to be left to a jury to decide whether Maria Hnatiuk had been in her right mind when she killed the only person who had cared enough to befriend her.

Her trial began at Norwich Crown Court on November 11th, 1996, when she admitted manslaughter on the grounds of diminished responsibility but denied murder.

Mr. David Stokes, prosecuting, told the jury that Maria Hnatiuk had a sexual interest in females and had stabbed Rachael Lean in the chest, back and throat, before leaving her face down in a copse.

"It was a frenzied attack," the prosecutor said. "Her heart was uninjured. It's likely that death did not occur immediately and may have taken several minutes. Her leggings had been pulled down revealing her buttocks. The Crown say that this was not done accidentally." He went on to say that the exposed buttocks might indicate "some sort of sexual motive towards killing Rachael." The wounds were of such severity that pathologists who performed the post-mortem said they were the worst they had ever seen.

Mr. Stokes said that Maria "insisted in twenty-three police interviews that she was not the killer. She said she had bumped into Rachael at the Naafi and left her to walk home alone... she is an accomplished liar. This was a calculating and wicked woman who killed a young woman on the threshold of life who had trusted her, and then pursued a false defence."

The court heard that Rachael's parents were separated but her mother lived in a nearby village and saw her regularly. Rachael had been due to go to Southampton University. "She had a regular boy friend," said Mr. Stokes, "and she enjoyed keeping fit, and went to the RAF gym on a regular basis."

It was there in August 1995, while waiting for the start of the new term, that she met and became friendly with Maria Hnatiuk, who was living locally with a man with whom she had a stormy relationship.

"They were known as the 'odd couple.' They had frequent rows and quarrels, leaving the defendant tearful and upset," said Mr. Stokes, adding that Hnatiuk and her boy friend had even drawn up a bizarre contract in which she promised never to speak to any other man. "There was a time when he seemed keen for her to bring home other women for sexual activities. The defendant was not adverse to such plans. She herself seemed to have sexual feelings towards women." But in the month before Rachael's death the couple split up, the man going to live with his parents.

Mr. Stokes said that the police had found letters, photographs and jottings written by Hnatiuk which were sexually explicit. Some were recovered from a village pond where she had thrown them. The jottings revealed "a particular interest in women's buttocks." One picture showed Maria Hnatiuk bending down and displaying her bottom.

The prosecutor emphasised that there was no suggestion that Rachael Lean had been interested in sexual activities with other women. On the day she vanished she had been seen walking with Maria Hnatiuk near the perimeter of RAF Coltishall, chatting amicably. Maria was seen later, sitting crying on the floor of the village telephone box.

It was significant, Mr. Stokes continued, that immediately after the killing Maria phoned her boy friend, who picked her up and drove her to London where she caught a train to Bristol, arriving at a relative's house with cut hands. She appeared to be "bright and chirpy" as she washed her bloodstained clothing and threw away the knife which had so brutally ended a young, innocent life.

Another witness told the court that on July 23rd, 1995, she attended the Buxton Carnival because her 11-year-old daughter was in it. "At about eight p.m. I went to the ladies' toilet. Just as I was about to close the door on the cubicle I heard a woman's voice say, 'I like your dress. You look lovely."

The witness said that the woman, who had bleached blonde hair, was still staring at her when she came out of the cubicle.

"The way she was looking at me made me feel very uncomfortable. She said to me, 'I was testing you to see how you would respond.'" Later the same woman approached her on the dance floor and spoke to her.

"She was complimenting me on my shape and the style of my hair. She asked where I worked and where I lived. She made me feel uncomfortable, as if she was trying to pick me up." The witness identified Maria Hnatiuk as the person.

Another witness said she met Maria Hnatiuk through a lesbian phone line in 1994. They went to a gay club together, and Maria later rang to ask if her own boy friend could come along too. "The way she was talking," the witness said, "she wanted a threesome sexually." The witness refused the suggestion.

In another statement which she made to the police, she admitted she had lesbian tendencies, and said she was seeking a sexual relationship with the right woman. But she claimed that her relationship with her boy friend was "fantastic." She told two women detectives: "It's the best I've ever had. I prefer being with a man than a woman, but I do have feelings for women. You are obviously heterosexual, so I wouldn't look at you sexually. It's only when I know there are lesbian or bisexual women around."

On the sixth day of the trial Maria Hnatiuk went into the witness box to tell her side of the story. She claimed that she had been dominated by an older man who encouraged her to "eliminate" five people in return for an offer of marriage. Now 29, she said she was dominated through violence and intimidation in every aspect of her life. The "older man" was 32 — hardly a huge age disparity.

Led by her counsel, Mr. Oliver Blunt QC, she said that her boy friend resented her pervious relationships. "He felt that the only way he would be happy was if those people weren't alive."

She claimed that he drew up a list of five people who had to be destroyed — four of her previous boy friends and one of his former girl friends. If she "eliminated" the first two he would allow her to go to the gym again. If she destroyed all five he would ask her to marry him. It must have been the most incredible claim ever made in Norwich Crown Court.

She agreed that she was "totally devoted" to the man despite his repeated physical abuse and psychological intimidation. She told the court that he was very confident and "more interesting and stimulating" than her previous boy friends. She alleged that he claimed to be a member of a covert organisation which sent him to Cambodia, and he told her he could get access to truth drugs and people who could harm her family. "I believed him. I was in fear."

She said that he moved her to "the middle of nowhere" — a series of villages outside Norwich — where she had no car, no money, and was "very isolated." He wanted her to be dominant in bed and fantasised aloud about her having lesbian sex.

"He felt he was dominant at work, so at home I was to be dominant in bed. He especially liked it if I dressed up in latex. He liked PVC and rubber." She said they had a normal sex life when they first met in 1991, but he became increasingly jealous of the previous men in her life.

"He then wanted me to be involved with a woman. That fantasy became a big thing." She told how he made her sign a contract in which she promised to bring women home for them both.

"It was about that time that he started hitting me," she claimed. "Infrequently at first, then every two or three days." She said she suffered black eyes and was not allowed to leave the house. She attempted suicide by taking an overdose of aspirin, and wrote him several letters describing herself as "a tart, scum and trash," which was how, she said, he made her feel.

Mr. Blunt then turned to the killing of Rachael, asking her to describe what she did.

"I got on well with Rachael," she said. "Very well. She was my friend." She claimed that her boy friend hated Rachael, whom he blamed for her contacts with other men. "He compared her to me. He said she had everything ahead of her and I had nothing. He went on and on every day. He hated her. Because of her I had gone out and broken every cardinal sin. He said if I hadn't met Rachael I'd never have met any of the men and been friendly."

She claimed that at the culmination of their four-year relationship he threw her out, forcing her to live rough, cut off her long blonde hair and watch him throw her belongings into a pond.

She was sleeping under a bush, living out of two carrier bags and eating snacks and fast food. She stole a ten-inch knife from a garden centre for protection and to cut her food. "I was really depressed," she said. "I was at the lowest point I had ever been, living rough with everyone looking at me as if I was a tramp. My life had no existence."

Describing her final meeting with Rachael, she said: "As we were walking Rachael was saying her father was in Bosnia, and that she was worried about him. She was saying about going to university and how she was looking forward to it."

"What was going through your mind?" asked her counsel.

Sobbing, she replied: "When we walked back I could see the lights of Coltishall and I thought I'm going back there to nothing. I just couldn't cope any more. It kept going round in my head what he had said about she's got to be dead, and if she's not dead you're going to have nothing.

"I pulled out the knife and started stabbing her. I stabbed her in the back. She turned around and called out my name and I just carried on. I stabbed her lots of times."

Mr. Blunt asked her why she had done this.

"Because she had to die. She had everything and I had nothing."

Asked about Rachael's leggings being pulled down to expose her bottom — which the prosecutor had called "the final indignity" — Maria Hnatiuk denied having done that. "I just remember dragging her by her hand and her ankles and putting her by a tree. Her leggings came down when I was pulling her."

At the end of her evidence her counsel told the jury that

there was "no rational explanation for Miss Lean's death. She was young, innocent, vibrant, on the threshold of her life and wholly undeserving of the manner of her death."

He went on: "The question is why? It is no consolation that there appears to be no rational explanation." Claiming that the only logical explanation was that Maria Hnatiuk had been brainwashed, he said: "This defendant was transformed from a pleasant, attractive, cheerful, outgoing girl to the figure described in this court: dishevelled, barefoot, cropped peroxide hair, lost, lonely and, in the words of a neighbour, rapidly going downhill."

Cross-examined by the prosecutor, Maria Hnatiuk expressed her remorse. "I feel very upset about what has happened to Rachael. I still can't believe what happened. I don't believe in violence."

She admitted that she intended to kill Rachael when she pulled out the knife. "I had the thought going round and round in my mind. It wasn't 'I am going to do this,' but him saying, 'You've got to do it.'"

She denied losing her temper after Rachael rejected her advances. "I wasn't in a temper," she said sadly. "She just had to die..."

In his closing speech Maria Hnatiuk's counsel told the jury that she had been suffering from such an abnormality of the mind as not to know the seriousness of what she was doing.

The prosecution argued that she knew perfectly well what she was doing, and her flight from the murder scene afterwards proved that she knew she had committed a serious crime and she intended to get away with it.

It took the jury just under four hours to reach their unanimous verdict of guilty of murder.

Maria Hnatiuk wept in the dock as Mr. Justice Blofeld sentenced her to life imprisonment. "This chilling murder was committed by you when you clearly knew what you were doing," he told her. "You deliberately chose, brutally, to end the life of Rachael Lean. She had done you no harm. She had been your friend. You killed her by repeatedly stabbing her. You then covered her body to prevent discovery, and thereafter lied and lied again.''

Maria Hnatiuk, wearing a white cardigan and black trousers, was then led sobbing from the dock by a prison officer. After she had been taken to the cells Rachael's father walked across the courtroom and hugged weeping women members of the jury, thanking each of them for convicting his daughter's killer.

He and his wife, with whom he had been reconciled, said that the last 14 months had been "sheer hell... this should have been an exciting time in our lives when we should have been sharing Rachael's adventures and experiences at university and comparing them with those of our friends. Now we can only wonder.

"There has been a lot of rain this year. If we could gather up all the tears for Rachael the world would have a new sea."

Detective Superintendent Steve Swain, who led the murder inquiry, said simply: "I am very pleased for the family... I think she has been rightly convicted of murder. I have no further thoughts about her, because all my thoughts are with the family."

But if what Maria Hnatiuk said about being dominated was even partly true, then one wonders. As anyone with the slightest knowledge of psychology will tell you, the easiest way to break someone is first to isolate them, and then continually tell them they are worthless. After a time they will reach breaking point... perhaps even kill ...

But what of the woman whose husband was devoted to her? Who worshipped the ground she stood on . . .

8

SEXUAL PERSUASION

Martin Lomax

"That woman is going to love you to death one day"

JOSE GARZA stretched out on the bed and gazed up at the ceiling. Folding his arms under his neck and flexing his stomach muscles. For a man approaching 50 Jose was feeling pretty good about life. A good job, loving children, and a sexy wife nearly 20 years younger than him. All of his colleagues told him what a fortunate guy he was, and he had no reason to argue. Jose was such a nice guy that everyone who knew him didn't envy him. Instead they were happy for him. If he came into the office in the morning looking tired and bleary eyed, most of the guys knew why. "That woman is going to love you to death one day, Jose," they would say, though they could never have known how close that joke was to being true.

Jose's mind was wandering off. He started to think about his heavy workload for the next day. Then the alluring scent of his wife's perfume brought him back to the present. The expectation of what was about to come caused him to stiffen, he wondered what position she would want to make love in that night. Nicole, his adoring wife, was so passionate and experimental that Jose sometimes wondered if he could always satisfy her. He would joke with her that she loved her kids like a mother, but she made love to him like a mistress. One thing was for sure, Jose wasn't complaining.

"I'm coming, honey, I hope you're ready," Nicole called out to him from the bathroom. Jose was ready all right, ready and waiting. The lights were out but the room was bathed in moonlight as she climbed under the sheets wearing a black negligee.

That night, Wednesday, September 25th, 1996, seemed like so many others in the two years since he and Nicole had moved to the quiet Los Angeles suburb of Sylmar. The two usually made love every evening, sometimes more than once. On that cool autumn evening Nicole seemed to be more turned on than usual. After their foreplay the two made frenzied love for about half an hour. By the time they were finished, the sheets and blankets were strewn all over the floor, the pillows had ended up at the foot of the bed along with Nicole's nightdress. The neighbourhood was so quiet, the couple used to wonder what the other residents could hear. No one ever complained — not that Jose would have been able to restrain his wife's passion even if he had wanted to.

As they lay entwined, panting heavily, the only sound that Jose could hear was his own heart pounding. Best exercise for a 51-year-old man I can think of, he mused to himself. And then just before eleven the dogs started barking. Polly and Rocky, their two Labradors, were very well trained. Jose knew they only barked if someone was nearby. Just as Jose was deliberating whether he should go downstairs the dogs fell silent. He rolled over and kissed his wife tenderly on the back of her neck.

It was turning into another perfect night for Jose. Home, then dinner, watch some TV with the family, put the kids to bed and read them a story and then "playtime," as Jose and his wife liked to call their love-making sessions. But a couple of minutes later the dogs started barking again, and then seconds later they stopped. Jose, a successful Los Angeles criminal prosecutor was in his own words, "a little spooked."

Jose would have been considerably more spooked if he had known what had set off the barking, because he was about to be thrust into a bizarre, terrifying series of incredible events that would shatter his life for ever. He knew none of this as he gently stroked Nicole's long auburn hair while massaging her shoulders.

When all was quiet again Nicole told Jose she was feeling peckish. "All that love-making sure gives me an appetite," she laughed, "I fancy eating something sweet," Jose said, "I'll get you an ice cream from the kitchen. I think I'll have one myself." Nicole stopped him as he got out of bed. She said, "No, Jose, can I have a low-fat yoghurt instead? Otherwise I'll get fat and you won't want me any more." Jose laughed, "O.K., whatever you want."

Getting his wife a yoghurt meant a trip to the garage for Jose, since Nicole's low-fat treats were kept in the big refrigerator there. He remembered that he was still feeling edgy from the barking. On impulse Jose, a gun collector and avid hunter, decided to take one of the two .45-calibre handguns that he kept loaded in his upstairs study. He padded quietly down the dark hallway past the rooms of their sleeping children, Richard 15 months, three-year-old Matthew, and their eldest child, Emily, who would be four the next day. She was so excited about her birthday that Jose thought she might still be awake, but there was no sound from her bedroom.

As he entered the two car garage he narrowly avoided falling over a wooden crate. The place was cluttered with junk: he was always promising to clear out the mess but somehow never got round to it. His left hand fumbled up and down the side wall until he found the light switch. With the lights on, he went straight to the fridge and took out two low-fat yoghurts, but instead of returning directly to the house some instinct made him step up to the front of the garage to check the doors.

Suddenly he heard several loud pops and looked down at his gun thinking that it might have gone off by accident. As he looked up again something seemed to flicker in the corner of his eye. In a split second he whipped his whole body round to the left, where he saw a hooded figure with tinted goggles standing about 12 feet away on the other side of his table tennis table, pointing a shiny silver .38 special straight at him.

Jose started screaming so loudly that the neighbours all recalled hearing him that night, despite the fact that all lived in detached houses. In an instant, he dropped the yoghurts, planted both his arms on the ping-pong table and fired off all five of his rounds from a crouching position. He heard the intruder grunt before slumping towards him as he crouched by the table.

Jose realised he was out of ammunition and ran back into the house. As he was half way down the hall he realised the door was still open, so he turned back and locked it. As he got to the foot of the stairs he saw Nicole standing outside the bedroom door with her hands clutching either side of her face. She kept shouting "Oh my God, oh my God." Her whole body was shaking.

"Get back inside the bedroom, lock the door and call 911. I've just shot someone in the garage."

Nicole screamed out, "No, no!" She didn't seem to grasp what was happening.

Then a noise distracted her from her shocked state. It was the little voice of her birthday girl, Emily. The other children had slept through the mayhem but Emily had got out of her bed and rushed to the door. "Mummy," she whispered timidly, "what's happening? I'm scared." As she started to cry Nicole picked her up and took her back into the main bedroom. By now the reality of what had happened was beginning to sink in with Jose. He went back to the garage door with his other fully loaded pistol. He knew that whoever he had shot wouldn't be going anywhere. What he didn't know was whether the intruder was dead or badly wounded.

Jose had seen more than his fair share of criminal cases during his prosecution work and thought that the worse was behind him. His beloved family were safe and his presence of mind had saved his own skin too. As it turned out, that night was only the beginning, and things were going to get far worse before they could ever be better again for poor Jose Garza and his family.

Within minutes two police cars were at the house in response to the 911 call. Then paramedics arrived and found the masked intruder face down in the garage. The armed robber was still alive, though with a very weak pulse; it was touch and go all the way to the hospital. After a gruelling three hour investigation by two detectives, Jose was relieved when they finished checking out his story.

When they told him the identity of his attacker Jose was dumbstruck. The mystery assailant was 34-year-old Lynette La Fontaine Trujillo, his wife's older sister. By now Jose was shaking uncontrollably. He looked over at Nicole. She sat on the sofa motionless her face had gone deathly pale. Jose wanted to ask her but couldn't. What the hell was his sister-in-law doing in his garage in the middle of the night with a gun and a mask? It wasn't only Jose who couldn't figure it out. The cops were pretty puzzled as well. But Nicole had a birthday party to run. Emily would have a nice time even after the tragedy. Jose didn't seem to have his heart in the party for one reason or another. Lynette died 12 days later from internal bleeding from two bullet wounds in her stomach. She never regained consciousness, so someone else was going to have to provide the answers.

Jose knew that Lynette, a divorced waitress and mother of four, had had her share of problems. She was jealous of her more successful sister who was a civil lawyer. She suffered lengthy and largely unsuccessful battles with bulimia and drugs and as a consequence her children were being cared for by their fathers. Ryan, 10, nine-year-old Spencer and six-year-old Travis lived with her ex-husband

Bill. Her ex-boyfriend, Sam Miller, looked after their three-year-old son Cody.

Though she'd had periods of mental instability during her life, Jose still wondered why his sister-in-law would want to kill him. What could she possibly gain by doing that? He was still trying to work it out when two days later half a dozen police officers arrived at his house at seven in the morning. As they came in, Nicole walked downstairs. The cops walked past Jose and surrounded his wife. "You are under arrest," one began as they handcuffed her and read her her rights.

Jose later recalled, "At that moment my whole world came crashing down on me. This nightmare wasn't going away, it was just getting worse. My first instinct was to call a lawyer for Nicole. I was angry that they had arrested her, I kept telling them that they were making a big mistake." At first Jose refused to believe that his adoring wife wanted him dead. But once the police laid out the vital evidence that they had found in Lynette's car the prosecutor in him couldn't deny it. It was literally put before him in black and white.

There on his coffee table, were a series of ripped up hand written and computer printed notes. On them were chilling instructions that Nicole had given her sister on how to murder Jose. *"Several shots to the back of the head,"* read one, as well as dozen of reasons for doing so. Among them were, *"Daily sexual abuse of your sister"* and *"Wasting childrens' resources on fishing, hunting and ham radio stuff,"* ... *"I can't have the family over when I want."*

The note concluded with a chilling message and the promise of better things to come. Nicole wrote, *"We have acted for years with men, and we are good at it. 90 seconds of terror and a complete turn around in your life. This will get you out of debt, pay for your boob operation, get you off the drugs, get you on Prozac and help you find a profession that you'll enjoy."*

The documents were dynamite for the prosecution. Dale Cutler, the deputy district attorney who led the case, remarked, "If we hadn't found that ball of paper, we would never have traced it to Nicole. She knew she was done for as soon as she knew the handwritten notes had not been destroyed by her sister. For such an intelligent, crafty lady she sure was careless."

Although the paper trail provided the who, it didn't really supply the why. The authorities usually find a strong motive comes to the fore at some time in an inquiry, and usually pretty early. This didn't prove to be the case this time.

Police uncovered no evidence to suggest that Jose had ever mistreated his wife, either physically or mentally. Even close relatives of the sisters, who had been brought up just a few miles away in the San Fernando Valley by their divorced mother, had no knowledge of any problems between the couple. "We really had no clue that this could ever happen," said the sister's aunt, April Murray, a Los Angeles high-school teacher. "So when it did, the family were asking, 'Who are these two girls?'"

Certainly the Nicole who emerges from the incriminating notes bears little resemblance to the "model kind of mother" that neighbour Stella Mondoza remembers making hot dogs for all the kids on the street on summer weekends. And she seems to be nothing like the "nice, warm person" who caught the eye of twice divorced Jose in a San Fernando Valley courtroom back in September 1991.

Nearly a year after the shooting Jose was still confused. He told a reporter, "I am still very much in love with the person that I met, if not the person she seemed become." On his answering machine at home he left a message saying he would accept reverse charged calls from Nicole while he is out. After Nicole went to jail she would call home as often as she was allowed, almost daily, and Jose and the kids would talk to her whenever possible. Emily, the eldest child, in particular misses her mother and remembers her fourth birthday party. Friends of the family who attended the party have said that Nicole gave an Oscar winning performance of an innocent wife and worried sister that day.

Jose says that he can't hate his wife. Since that fateful day he has struggled desperately to explain how Nicole's "complete aberration" happened. The most plausible reason he feels is that his wife became unbalanced by a cocktail of diet pills that she was taking every day. He maintains that she lost nearly three stone in weight in the six months before she tried to have him killed.

Less charitably, others believe that behind the veneer of a model wife Nicole, who had rebounded from a brief and disastrous early marriage to put herself through law school, had much in common with her more overtly troubled older sister. Their mother, Cynthia Berken, a retired elementary school-teacher, suggested that her own lengthy illnesses during the girls' childhood, in particular a serious bout of colitis that forced her to spend a year in hospital when Nicole was only three, had badly disrupted the sisters' upbringing. During that time the girls were sent to stay with their absentee father, who was more concerned about having beer in the fridge than food on the table.

Kathleen Uzanov, an acclaimed clinical psychologist who has given evidence in many criminal cases, said, "Children who have to learn to survive by themselves early on in life may not develop empathy and concern for others. It is proven that they can be very charming and manipulative. They can often be quite intelligent and over-achievers. The other side of the coin is that they lack remorse or guilt for their actions and will be looking out for themselves and taking care of number one."

In the curious case of Lynette and Nicole, all this seems likely to remain speculation and at best educated guess-work. The fact is that Lynette can't speak for herself and Nicole won't. Because Nicole chose to plead no contest to reduced charges of voluntary manslaughter and attempted murder in January 1997, before a preliminary hearing could be arranged, her story may never be known.

Sandra and Bob
Wignall on their
wedding day.
Chapter 13

Body beautiful. Sally McNeil and her husband,
Mr. California

Ethel Anne Trigwell. Death of a Private Eye. Chapter 15

Nita Carter (above) was described as, "the Devil Bitch from Hell." Chapter 18

Barbara Bell. Accident or cold-blooded murder? Chapter 16

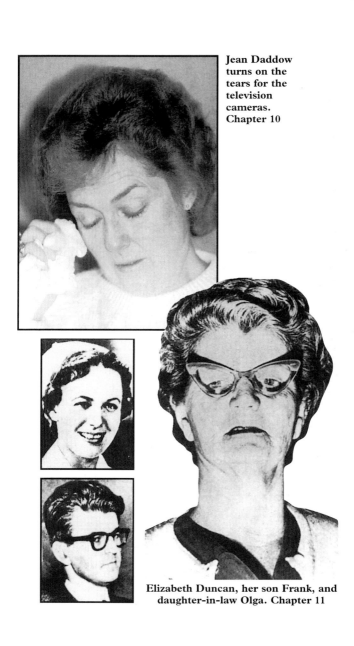

Jean Daddow turns on the tears for the television cameras. Chapter 10

Elizabeth Duncan, her son Frank, and daughter-in-law Olga. Chapter 11

Jean Lee and her cohorts in crime, Bobby Clayton (top) and Norman Andrews. Chapter 12

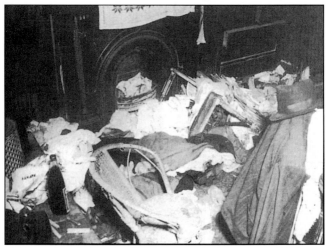

Pop's front room as the police found it. Chapter 12

One time model Omaima
Nelson and her unfortunate
husband Bill. Chapter 1

Diana Haun. She
beheaded her victim
in the name of love.
Chapter 2

The crying game.
Above, Tracie
Andrews at a
press conference
and right, Rhonda
Belle Martin
during an
interview on
Death Row.
Chapters 3 and 4

Sisters Nicole and Lynette Garza. Chapter 8

Betty Broderick. Someone suggested that the newly-weds should wear bullet-proof vests. Chapter 9

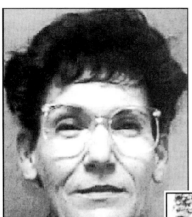

Above, Judy Buenoano and below, the shrivelled hands of one of her victims. Chapter 5

Maria Hnatiuk.
A shocking
murder in
Norfolk.
Chapter 7

What is certain is that little Emily Garza will be 16 before her mother becomes eligible for parole. For years Nicole would swop her comfortable suburban home for a 6 by 10 foot cell at the state prison in Chowchilla, California. Although the jail is more than a five-hour drive from Sylmar, Jose has vowed to take the kids to see their mother once a month for as long as she is there. Jose has described Nicole as distraught and apologetic, though she has never attempted to explain her behaviour. He said, "She has never come out and said, 'I wanted you dead,' sometimes she still tells me she loves me."

In fact Jose feels that he has lost almost as much as his wife and her sister. "I tell her three things," he says, "the kids love you, I love you, and we will never abandon you. I feel I am a prisoner with her."

9

A HIGH DEGREE OF CALLOUSNESS

Don Lasseter

Someone suggested that the newly-weds should wear bullet-proof vests

PRE-DAWN darkness dampened by a lingering ocean mist shrouded the Georgian-style mansion. Inside, a shadowy figure silently climbed the stairs.

Dan and Linda Broderick heard nothing as they slept in their upstairs master bedroom. They had planned to sleep in on Sunday morning, November 5th, 1989, in the quiet San Diego suburb of Clairmont. A rear door to the bedroom opened silently allowing the intruder to enter near the headboard of the double bed and look down upon the sleeping couple.

Linda was curled next to her husband of less than seven months. They were an attractive couple in the prime of their lives ... lives that would last just a few minutes more.

A creaking floor board stirred Dan from his sleep, and when he moved Linda also opened her eyes. They saw the intruder simultaneously. Linda screamed as Dan lunged for the bedside telephone.

At that point the dark bedroom exploded as orange blasts and black smoke erupted from the .38-calibre Smith and Wesson five-shot revolver in the grip of the intruder.

One of the "Hydra Shock" cartridges — designed to inflict maximum tissue damage — slammed into the middle of Dan Broderick's back. His right lung was shredded and a rib shattered, leaving him crumpled on the floor next to the bed, drowning in his own blood.

Four more shots thundered within the room. One hit a bedside table near Dan, another smashed into the wall above the bed. The final two bullets tore into Linda Broderick, killing her instantly. One entered the base of her skull from the back, lodging in her brain, the other tore into her chest.

The telephone lay near Dan's hand, so the intruder stepped over him, grabbed the phone and ripped the cord from the wall. Meanwhile, Dan lay still, his life draining away.

At 7.30 a.m. an attorney and a good friend of Dan Broderick, who lived only a short distance away, received a visitor, a man who also knew Dan. The visitor, Vern Curry, had tried unsuccessfully to telephone the Broderick residence several times and had become alarmed.

The two men drove the short distance to the Broderick home and knocked. There was no response, and the door was locked. At the rear of the house, which overlooked a Forest canyon, the men found the back door also locked. Finding a window open, the two men climbed in.

Morning light filtered through the windows in the deathly quiet house. The men, feeling apprehensive, searched the ground floor but found nothing disturbed. Cautiously they ascended the stairs. Despite danger alarms buzzing in their heads, they proceeded into the bedroom.

When they saw Linda Broderick face down on the bed and Dan lying prone on the floor they froze. When the horrible reality dawned on them the attorney rushed over to the bodies to check for signs of life, but both Dan and Linda were dead.

Detective Sergeant Tom Callaway was assigned to the case just before 8 a.m. on Sunday. He called out his investigators and sped to the scene.

One of the first tasks was to examine the bodies and the scene and to talk to the two men who had made the grim discovery.

The men told Detective Zavala how they had tried to contact the Brodericks by telephone and couldn't. When they had arrived at the house all the exterior doors had been locked, so they had been forced to open a window to enter the dwelling.

Detective Zavala then conferred with Callaway. The killer had not entered through a window, and all the doors had been locked. There were no other signs of forced entry. The killer had apparently used a key and had carefully locked the door when he fled.

The time of the shooting was established by two neighbours. They reported hearing gunshots at 5 a.m.

When the detectives first learned that Dan Broderick's fortune had been made suing doctors, they wondered if a lawsuit victim had obtained a key to his house and killed him.

Meanwhile, with the help of the attorney interviewed by Detective Zavala and through other witnesses the investigators learned about the backgrounds of Daniel Thomas Broderick III and his recent bride, Linda Bernadette Kolkena Broderick.

The attorney friend had known Dan Broderick since 1973 when they both worked for the same law firm. Dan's rise to fame and fortune had been meteoric in the wealthy beach town of La Jolla, just north of San Diego.

After graduating from Cornell School of Medicine and Harvard Law School, Dan had decided to focus his legal career on medical malpractice. It proved to be a fertile field to harvest; Dan was reported to have been making more than a million dollars annually. His recent marriage to Linda was his second matrimonial tie.

In the mid-1960s, gawky young Dan Broderick, sporting sideburns and round tortoiseshell glasses, was attending the University of Notre Dame. At a party he was enchanted by an attractive blonde named Elizabeth who was visiting from Mount Saint Vincent School in New York. Dan was fascinated. He kept in contact with Elizabeth after she returned to New Manhattan, and in fact he intensified his pursuit of her.

Elizabeth Ann was from an affluent Catholic New York family who believed that work was necessary to achieve anything in life. So while she had many advantages, she also worked, frequently as a model.

The relationship between Elizabeth and Dan flowered during the late '60s while they both continued their studies. Money was tight for Dan, so Elizabeth paid for most of their dates. Also, Dan didn't have a car, so they used hers. But it didn't seem to matter; they were young and in love.

After Elizabeth graduated with a degree in education, Dan finally asked her to marry him even though he was still facing the rigours of medical school. Elizabeth accepted, and in April, 1969, they were wed at the Immaculate Conception Church. He would call his bride Betty.

Dan's parents were able to pay for his education and his food and lodging, but there was not an excess of money available. Betty learned that she was going to have to modify her previous lifestyle. There would be no more maids, no more expensive clothing and country clubs. Just a tiny dormitory room at Dan's school, a room in which Betty was expected to scrub, cook and clean.

Betty was the victim of a culture shock. She considered leaving Dan early in the marriage, but when she found that she was pregnant she decided to stay. She would eventually bear him four children.

Following his stint at medical school, Dan decided to shift to the legal profession where he could specialise in litigation in the medical field.

After his graduation from Harvard and the birth of their second child, and after enduring what Betty regarded as endless problems and privation, the growing family moved to San Diego, California, in 1973.

In Southern California, where the courts are jammed with lawsuits, Dan Broderick's skills and knowledge proved to be a gold mine. He rapidly established a reputation as a successful lawyer, one whom people began to see as a community leader.

Success in the courtroom also bred success on the social ladder. The Brodericks moved in 1976 to La Jolla, where the ocean view was magnificent, the homes beautiful and the social circles populated with the rich and famous.

Two years later Dan left his job at the law firm to establish his own practice. Country club memberships followed, along with luxury cars, a private swimming pool, first-class holidays and private education for the children. Dan even became president of the local bar association. Betty Broderick had at last recovered — perhaps even exceeded — her former lifestyle.

But the good life had its pitfalls, Dan and Betty began to argue, first about minor things, then about everything. Dan's interests and activities increasingly centered on his work, while Betty retreated into bickering with the children and threatening to end the marriage. More and more Dan found reasons to be at the office.

In 1983 he decided that he needed some office help in his rented luxury suite in a building that catered for attorneys. He took on Linda Kolkena, 22, who had recently left her job at Delta Airlines.

There was soon open gossip that an affair was blossoming between the lovely Linda Kolkena and Dan Broderick. One acquaintance later admitted that he'd let Linda and Dan use a hotel room where he himself worked during the latter part of 1983 "on several occasions."

All the talk inevitably found its way to Betty Broderick, and she became suspicious and angry. Dan denied everything.

On Dan's birthday, November 11th, 1983, Betty went to his office for a surprise celebration and found that a party had already started much earlier in Linda Kolkena's office. Dan and Linda, however, had left. Betty waited, but the pair never returned. Finally, Betty went home, piled most of Dan's clothes in a heap in the back garden, and set them on fire.

Acrimony between the couple escalated. On one trip to New York Dan told Betty that he didn't love her any more.

Back in San Diego, Dan moved Betty and the children into a rented house while their home was being repaired. A few months later, Dan moved back to the home, alone. Furious, Betty drove to the home and indulged in a destructive binge. She broke glass, shattered mirrors and spray-painted graffiti on the walls. Dan filed for divorce the following September.

The divorce proceedings were a war for the next five years. Betty, fearful of Dan's power in the legal system and frustrated by the lack of ability to compete on an equal footing, became more and more unsettled.

Dan Broderick wanted to sell the home in which he was living, but Betty refused to sign the papers. He resorted, at last, to an unusual procedure wherein a judge signed an order for the sale and it sold for a low price.

Betty was outraged, even though Dan bought her a new ocean-view home in La Jolla for $650,000. Dan also providing monthly income for her that started at $9,000 and eventually increased to more than $16,000.

Despite the teaching credentials and the licence she had, Betty did not choose to work. She seemed to be totally consumed by what she regarded as unfair treatment from Dan. She did, however, find time for a male companion.

Dan purchased the luxury home in Marston Hills, and in April, 1989, shortly after his divorce was final, he married Linda Kolkena there in a front-lawn ceremony. The ex-Mrs. Broderick was not invited, and someone suggested — not completely in jest — that the newly-weds should wear bulletproof vests.

The detectives looking for clues at the murder scene still wondered if a disgruntled doctor whom Dan had ruined in a malpractice suit had wreaked revenge. But they mostly wanted to talk to Betty Broderick. And when Detective

Mathena interviewed Vern Curry — one of the men who had discovered the bodies of Dan and Linda Broderick — the need to interview Betty became even more urgent.

Apparently, Vern and Betty had been lovers for several years. On Saturday evening — the night before the murders — Betty had invited Vern to her La Jolle home for dinner.

"She seemed calm that evening," Curry told Detective Mathena. "She and I had just returned from a four-day trip to Acapulco the previous weekend."

Then Vern Curry dropped the bombshell. On Sunday morning, at 7 o'clock on the morning of the murders, Curry had received a phone call from a Tania Stone, a friend of Betty Broderick.

"Betty just phoned me," Tania had said, "and she told me she had been over to Dan and Linda's house."

Curry had been asleep when the call came and was still a little groggy, but Tania soon woke him up.

"Vern, Betty said she had a gun with her and some shots were fired," Tania said. "She was calling me from a phone box. She was saying something about she had contemplated committing suicide, but she didn't have enough bullets left in the gun or something."

"Where was she calling from?" Curry had demanded to know.

"I wasn't sure," Tania replied. "Probably somewhere in Clairmont."

Vern Curry, who lived close to the Broderick house, had first tried to call Dan. Getting no reply, he raced over to the house of the attorney who was Dan's friend, and the two of them went to the Broderick home where they made the grisly discovery.

"I knew she had a gun," Curry told Detective Mathena. "She mentioned, you know, she had fired a gun and that she was pretty good at it."

Detective Richard Allen was dispatched by Sergeant Callaway to Pacific Beach to interview a relative of Betty Broderick. She told the detective that Betty had phoned her on Sunday morning, awakening her around 6.30 a.m. Detective Allen noted that the call came well within two hours of the murders.

She said Betty had told her she was in trouble. "Betty also left her handbag here," the relative told Allen. "I saw a gun in it."

Detective Allen looked into the handbag and saw a five-shot Smith and Wesson .38-calibre pistol. With the relative's permission, he took the gun with him when he left.

Later questioned at length, the relative added many details to her story about her contact with Betty Broderick that Sunday morning.

When Betty first called with her astonishing message, she had whispered, "I'm in a telephone box in Clairmont. I'm in trouble, I'm coming over. I shot Dan, I shot the sonofabitch, and I'm on my way over to your house.

"If I don't show up," Betty continued, "the cops will have found me." She then hung up.

Some 10 minutes later Betty Broderick arrived at her relative's apartment and blurted out, "I shot Dan!"

Frantic, the younger woman asked, "Where? How many times? What did he say?"

"I don't know," Betty replied. "I don't know if I really shot him. It was dark. I didn't hear anyone scream, but Dan said, 'Okay, you shot me. I'm dead.' Then he fell off the bed."

The young woman continued quoting the statements that Betty Broderick had made to her. "She told me that she ripped the phone off the wall."

"Do you know how she got in the house?"

"She said she tried the front door and it wouldn't open so she went round to the back and used a key to open the door. She went straight upstairs, through the TV room and into their bedroom.

Continuing her account of Betty's nervous rambling, the woman said that Betty had got the key from one of her children. Dan had recently changed all the locks to make sure that Betty could not get into the house, but he had given a key to his daughter. Betty had obtained that key.

"She wanted me to go to the house and check to see if her two sons, who lived with Dan and Linda, were okay," the relative said. "she also said that Dan had sent her papers the night before that would put her in jail."

"What happened next?"

"Well, my boy friend and I left Betty in the apartment and drove over to Dan's house to check on the boys." The woman admitted that Betty had also asked her to look for a security box with some papers Betty wanted and a personal phone book.

"The police were swarming all over the place, and they asked if I had seen Betty Broderick. I said no, I hadn't seen her, that I was there to pick up my laundry, and we left."

The girl and her boy friend returned to the apartment and found Betty still there. After Betty made several phone calls, the trio discussed what to do. They decided to take Betty to the police station so she could surrender herself. They drove, the relative said, to the San Diego police station in La Jolla. On the way they picked up Betty's friend Tania Stone, and were followed by another female friend of Betty.

At the police station the five of them sat outside and talked for a while. They finally decided that Betty should call an attorney before she voluntarily surrendered to the police. Betty asked her relative to go to her house, pick up some diaries, a phone book and some personal index cards and then return to the police station. Meanwhile, Betty went to find a phone box. The friend who had followed them waited with her while the other three left to run the errand for Betty.

At Betty's residence the trio were surprised to see Detective Allen and some of the other officers who were at Dan Broderick's house earlier. The relative later admitted that "the officers thought it strange that we had been to both places, so they asked us to go downtown with them, and we did."

In the police station the young relative answered more questions. Yes, she had seen the gun from Betty's handbag before. Betty had once said, "I keep it in my pocket, and if Dan gives me any trouble I'm going to get him." The relative added that she had gone shopping with Betty the Friday before the shooting and Betty had not seemed angry or upset then.

Tania Stone, the friend of Betty Broderick who had called Vern Curry to alert him to Betty's strange phone call, was also interviewed.

"Yes, Betty called me some time between six or seven on Sunday morning. I think it was from a phone box in Clairmont."

"I need help," Betty had said. "I don't know why I'm calling you. I'm sick, nauseous and upset, and I need to be with somebody. I just came from Dan's house, and I may have shot somebody. It was dark and I couldn't see anything."

Then, Tania Stone reported, Betty said, "If there was another bullet in the gun I would have used it on myself."

In a phone box close to the police station Betty Broderick began to call attorneys, but it was Sunday and she was having trouble reaching anyone. Finally she contacted a lawyer who agreed to meet her and Betty left in the car with the friend who had waited with her.

Later in the day Betty walked into the police station with her attorney and voluntarily surrendered.

The news coverage on the murders and the arrest of Betty Broderick hit the headlines the following morning and continued for the next two years. Headlines, extensive stories in Sunday magazines, TV chat shows and even a full-length TV movie revealed every detail of Betty and Dan Broderick's lives and the murders. The public couldn't seem to hear enough about it.

Betty would later say on a TV chat show that some of the details in the movie weren't accurate. "Some things obviously happened," she said. "One out of five things happened. Of the rest, there was no evidence of anyone ever doing those things."

One particular event was repeatedly shown. In a fit of temper Betty had driven her red and grey 1987 Chevrolet across the lawn of Dan and Linda's home and smashed into the front door. On that incident, Betty later said, "Everyone is making such a big deal about me driving my car through his house. If I had wanted to drive my car through his house I easily could have done it. I mean, they've made such a big deal about it ..."

Betty was also accused of frequently making obscene and threatening phone calls to Dan and Linda and leaving messages on their answering machine.

On one such message — used later in court — she said, "You have one hell of a nerve dumping the kids here on the pavement and zooming away without making any attempt to communicate with me about my plans for the weekend. You make me sick, both of you. I have very important things to ask you, but you've made me mad. I'll kill you!"

Betty's fluctuating weight also became an issue. Her trim figure began to bloat in the months leading up to the shooting. She said that Dan had called her "old and fat" and compared her unfavourably to the slim young Linda. There was also a considerable age difference between the two women. Betty was 42, Linda only 28.

Meanwhile, the detectives continued to investigate, searching for evidence to use against Betty Broderick in her pending murder trial. They located several friends of the victims who said that Betty had made numerous threats to kill both Dan and Linda.

While Betty was telling her attorneys (she sacked two before the case ever reached trial) that she was the victim of Dan's financial manipulation and harassment, some people were pointing out that she was the one who originated much of the harassment. It became so intensive, friends said, that Dan resorted to withholding money — $100 up to $1,000 — from Betty's monthly allotment as "fines" for her behaviour.

Betty claimed that she had gone to the Broderick home to commit suicide in front of Dan and Linda. She said she had even written a suicide note and left it at home. But detectives had thoroughly searched Betty's residence and no suicide note was ever found. Nothing turned up either in a search of the car Betty drove.

Kerry Wells, a deputy district attorney for San Diego County, prosecuted Betty Broderick for first-degree murder. The trial began in June, 1990, and lasted several months.

Defence Attorney Jack Early presented a case that characterised Betty Broderick as a mentally battered woman who was driven to her desperate act. She had no intention of killing the couple, he contended. On the contrary, "Dan was even thinking of killing *her* if he had to. He was trying to make her penniless and told a number of people it wouldn't be over until one of them was gone."

Earley informed the jury that Dan Broderick had told Betty in regard to the divorce proceedings, "Okay, if you want to fight, you're going to be in the ring with Muhammad Ali. You're going to be in here with a heavyweight. We're going to litigate this case the hardest way we can."

Defence Attorney Earley argued that Betty "was left in a state of depression, and the anger was as much at herself as anyone else. She couldn't dig herself out from under the avalanche. She could never escape, and it still haunts her."

However, many observers couldn't see a beautiful ocean-view home, $16,000 a month and a life of luxury as anything to be depressed about.

Ten members of the jury rejected Jack Earley's defence and accepted Prosecutor Kerry Wells's arguments. They voted to convict Betty of first-degree murder. However, two of the jurors insisted that Betty was guilty of nothing more than manslaughter. No compromise could be reached, and they announced to a crowded courtroom that they were a hung jury. The judge had no choice but to declare a mistrial.

The second trial began in October, 1991, with the same team of lawyers before Superior Court Judge Thomas Whelan.

Eight weeks later the jury began their deliberations while the news media and millions of people waited breathlessly. When the jury emerged on December 10th they delivered a verdict of "guilty of murder in the second degree."

Betty, who had demonstrated an occasional tendency to histrionics, smiled pleasantly at the jurors as they were individually polled. Prosecutor Wells too smiled, and hugged her husband. Jack Earley said he would appeal.

The jury foreman said that throughout the deliberations, "We thought we would have a hung jury. We all had sympathy for her and felt it was a tremendous tragedy. But we saw so much aberrant behaviour. Her reactions weren't something a normal, reasonable person would do."

On February 7th, 1992, Judge Whelan described the case as "a tragedy from start to finish." Betty Broderick, he said, showed a "high degree of callousness" when she shot Dan and Linda Broderick to death and left her ex-husband lying "gurgling in his own blood."

Judge Whelan then sentenced Betty Broderick to 32 years in prison, the maximum term possible for her conviction. She must serve at least 18 years before she can be considered for parole.

10
THE BLACK WIDOW

Brian Marriner

**"Treasured memories of Terence John
Daddow. Taken suddenly on 26 November,
1991, aged 52 years. In God's house but in
my heart, your wife Jean."**

The Black Widow spider is so named because after
luring her male to her treacherous web, and immediately after the act of mating, she kills and devours
him. Jean Daddow is not only a Black Widow in this sense,
but she spun a web into which she lured and trapped
others in a cunning and sordid murder plot. She is
arguably Britain's most cold-blooded and ruthless female
killer of present times. Greed was the sticky substance she
used to entrap others in her web, but the venom was hers
alone. She was pure poison.

There is evidence that she planned to murder her
husband even before she married him.

It was at 10.30 p.m. on November 26th, 1991, when
retired banker Terry Daddow answered a knock at the
front door of his luxury cottage home in the East Sussex
village of Northiam, near Rye. Although it was late evening
Mr. Daddow felt no alarm, assuming it was a neighbour
wanting something. But it was nemesis. Daddow just had
time to register the stranger on his doorstep, dressed in

black, before a single blast from a 12-bore shotgun almost tore his heart out. Hurled backwards by the impact, he collapsed in the hall of his home, his head at the bottom of the stairs.

As he lay there, blood pouring from his mouth, his eyes glazing over, his wife waited in an upstairs bedroom. Fifteen minutes passed before she phoned the police. She was to claim later that the delay was due to shock, but detectives had another explanation. It was to give the hired killer time to get away.

Then police arrived at Chapelfield Cottage quickly, taking a statement from the wife while waiting for the pathologist to come and make his examination. Forensic technicians searched the murder scene meticulously, and photographs of the body were taken from all angles. It was after midnight before the body of Terry Daddow, 52, was removed to the mortuary.

Detective Superintendent Brian Foster immediately took a close look at the wife — not just because the closest relative automatically becomes the prime suspect in such situations, but also because it was apparent from the start that something very odd had been going on.

On the day Daddow died, a strange and garbled advertisement placed by the victim had appeared in the local newspaper, the *Wealdon Advertiser*.

It read:

"DADDOW, TERRY, JEAN. Because of malicious gossip would like it known they are happily married and together. All have been proved by solicitors etc, not guilty of fraud, theft or senility. Thanks to the few true friends who believed in us, perhaps the rest could find themselves to criticise or work for their sick minds."

In the first few weeks following the murder the police routinely followed several leads, the majority of which proved to be dead-ends. Most of the detective work went into researching Terry Daddow's background. Such inquiries often yield a clue to the killing. They will usually turn up a motive, and once the police have that, it often leads to the killer. When faced with an apparently senseless murder, the experienced detective asks himself "Who benefits?" and "Who has a motive?"

It soon became clear that Terry Daddow had been no saint. A former assistant bank manager in nearby Tenterden, he was the second husband of Jean Daddow, the marriage taking place on June 6th, 1989, at Gretna Green, the traditional spot for runaway teenagers. Yet Terry Daddow had been 50, and Jean Blackman only a year younger . . .

The couple first met in 1985, when Terry Daddow, a respectable married man with three sons, was both an assistant bank manager and a financial investment adviser. Jean Blackman, who had enjoyed a string of lovers, was in business as a hairdresser in Tenterden and went to the bank in some distress because her credit cards had been stolen. Then aged 45, she wore short skirts and plunging necklines. She also used rather too much eye-shadow to hide the signs of advancing years.

It began as a friendly relationship, with Terry Daddow giving both Jean and her husband financial advice, but it quickly ripened into a full-blown affair, with the bank manager writing torrid poetry to his client and phoning her from work at every opportunity.

When middle-aged men begin an affair it is usually a recipe for disaster. They fall as badly as any love-sick teenager, convincing themselves that this is the one great passion in their lives. Jean found it easy to steal Terry from his wife and three sons. Her own marriage was crumbling anyway, and she was looking for a new nest. A bank manager would do nicely . . .

Terry Daddow left his wife and moved in with the Blackmans at Royal Cottage in Biddenden, as a lodger. Police were to discover that it was not the first time that Jean Blackman had moved her lovers into her home as "lodgers." Detectives questioned half a dozen men who had been her "lodgers" over the years.

Terry Daddow made the mistake of confiding to his

mistress that he was making a fortune from fleecing elderly women. They trusted him as a financial adviser and almost fell over themselves to give him money. One woman, moved by his tales of personal hardship, promised to leave him her £250,000 house in her will, and another paid for him to take an expensive foreign holiday. Others bought him cars. Terry Daddow was a glib con-man.

Jean Blackman began working with him on his money-making schemes, parting lonely and confused old women from their life-savings. One 81-year-old childless widow, twice gave the couple £3,000 to buy second hand cars. She also loaned them £10,000 to cover the legal costs of suing a builder for work done in their home. That "loan" was never repaid. "He had great charm," the widow later said. "He always seemed to be suffering misfortunes and I felt sorry for him."

However, the relationship between the plundering couple became so intense that Terry Daddow began drinking heavily, and began suffering from severe stress when gossip and ugly rumours surfaced about his activities. He was subjected to a Fraud Squad inquiry. No charges were brought — there was no proof, and there is no law against elderly women giving their money away — but after medical advice, and because he kept taking extended sick leave, in May, 1990, Daddow was forced to take early retirement after 28 years with the bank. Jean Daddow had not planned to live with a pensioner.

In February, 1990, the couple bought Chapelfield Cottage in Dixler Road in Northiam, paying £162,000 for the property. That money did not come from any golden handshake. It was a gift from a 92-year-old widow for whom Terry Daddow had often done accountancy work. Denying that she was senile, she said she had given the couple the money because she wanted to help them make their new marriage work, and felt that a new start in a new house would be the best way to do it. A lot more money was spent on decorating the cottage and buying furniture.

The widow's relatives objected to her cash gift to Daddow, feeling that she was no longer competent to handle her finances. Her nephew turned amateur detective in an attempt to expose Daddow as a con-man, incurring the enmity of the Daddows in the process. It was he who had unearthed the earlier investigation into Daddow's activities. But the old lady had put the business of overseeing the gift into the hands of her solicitors, and everything seemed lawful and watertight.

That cash gift was not the only money that Terry Daddow had received. Detectives often heard rumours that the couple had been conning old people into handing over their savings. It was estimated that they might have received as much as half a million pounds in this way.

Once married, Jean Daddow expertly spun her web around her besotted husband. It was ironic that the master con-man should himself have been conned — a case of the biter being bit. At first there was sex and plenty of it, torrid sex that made Terry feel like a young man again. Detectives searching the cottage where Terry had been murdered uncovered nude snaps of the pair, and the many kinky letters which Terry had written to Jean during their short courtship and three-year marriage.

What people do in the privacy of their bedrooms, however, is not the business of the law. Yet this material was a stark contrast to the image the couple projected — when they first moved into the cottage, neighbours nicknamed them "Terry and June" because they looked just like the demure suburban couple in the popular television sitcom.

The police, who had been baffled by the source of Terry Daddow's wealth, now had to consider the possibility that he had been murdered by a former client or associate harbouring a grudge. This was to prove to be another false trail, but Detective Superintendent Brian Foster was later to say, "We began to find out that the quiet, middle-aged Daddows weren't all they had seemed ... Detectives were investigating leads in all sorts of directions and by pooling information and by using a computer, a pattern began to emerge — and it centred upon Jean Daddow."

Once she had Terry hopelessly enmeshed, Jean set about putting the rest of her plan into operation. For months she would slip LSD into her husband's food to give him hallucinations and increase the depression to which he was prone and which had forced his early retirement. That advertisement in the *Wealdon Advertiser* shows his state of mind, reading like something concocted by a man who wasn't thinking coherently.

It was easy for Jean to persuade Terry to cut his former family out of his will and to make her the sole beneficiary. That done, she then gained control of the 30 different bank and building society accounts which Terry had established to squirrel away the cash he was receiving from elderly people for "investment."

To Jean Daddow, Terry represented a victim worth at least £300,000 — but only if he were dead.

According to a former girl friend of Jean Daddow's son from a previous marriage Jean once asked her son Roger Blackman if he knew anyone "who would kill Terry for £1,000." She posed this question even before her marriage to Daddow had taken place.

Instead of expressing surprise, Blackman told his mother that he knew people who would do it. The son recruited Robert Bell, 39, from Headcorn, Kent.

Bell was a former soldier; in his youth he had joined the Foreign Legion but had deserted.

For his "expertise" Bell demanded a hefty fee for killing the unwanted husband; he wanted £7,000 in cash. Reluctantly, Jean Daddow drew the money from the account she shared with Terry, handing the money over in a shoebox, and perhaps consoling herself with the thought that since it was a joint account, the victim was paying half the cost of his own execution.

It was in the carrying out of his murder plans that Bell revealed himself as the fantasist and bungler that he really was. During lengthy discussions and negotiations he was to think up 10 separate ways of killing Terry Daddow. These included beating him, shooting him from a car, shooting him with a crossbow, and forcibly injecting him with a drugs overdose. All these abortive attempts took place in the weeks before he finally got up the nerve to blast Daddow to death on his own doorstep with a shotgun supplied by Blackman. Even then he probably hoped that Terry Daddow would not answer his door bell so late at night . .

After the murder, Bell flew to America, and later phoned an English journalist to confess to the killing. He was persuaded to return to Britain by the police, and he arrived confident that he could talk his way out of trouble by casting the blame on Jean Daddow and her son.

Immediately after the murder Jean Daddow had appeared on television at a police press conference, acting as a grieving widow and begging the killer to give himself up. As part of her charade, she had her husband buried with a tombstone at his head reading:

"Treasured memories of Terence John Daddow. Taken suddenly on 26 November, 1991, aged 52 years. In God's house but in my heart, your wife Jean."

Questioned by detectives, she threw suspicion on the nephew of the old lady who had given the couple the money for their home, suggesting he was the likely killer. After all, she pointed out, he was the major beneficiary under the old lady's will since both her husband and their son had been killed on active service during World War II.

It was an inspired story, and it was taken seriously. In the early hours of November 27th, the phone rang at the nephew's three bedroomed house in Tenterden. It was answered by his 15-year-old son. On the line was a high-ranking police officer saying that the house was surrounded by armed police. The son was ordered to come out with his father and 18-year-old brother, with their hands above their heads.

Arrested on suspicion of murder and taken to a police

station for questioning, the nephew agreed that he had been unhappy about the money flowing from his auntie's bank account to the Daddows, and had shared his suspicions with the Fraud Squad at Canterbury. But he denied being behind the malicious slanders circulating in Tenterden about Terry Daddow fleecing old folk. And there was the matter of a cast-iron alibi . . .

At the time that Terry Daddow had been blasted to death, the old lady's nephew had been having a drink in his local pub in Tenterden . . . with the former Chief Constable of Kent.

He therefore walked free within hours.

When that plot failed, Jean Daddow planted a condom in her dead husband's car in an effort to suggest that a love rival or jealous husband might have been the killer.

Aware that the police were closing in on her, and that her arrest was imminent, she wrote a remarkable letter to a journalist who was researching the case and after posting it, took a massive drugs overdose. The letter's 32 hand-written pages, sealed in a manilla envelope, were posted on the morning of Friday, March 6th, 1992. Almost four months after the murder.

Jean Daddow was living at her parents' home in the Kent village of Biddenden and had walked a few yards to the post box before returning home to take the overdose. That letter was meant to be her suicide note. But she must have counted on being found by her parents before the drugs had a fatal effect.

Jean Daddow was discovered on top of her bed and was rushed to Maidstone Hospital. Her condition was described as "serious." The police waited until she was well enough, and then at the beginning of the following week, they charged her with conspiracy to murder her husband. Roger Blackman and Robert Bell were also charged, Bell being accused of having carried out the killing. All three were held at Hastings police station where they denied the charge.

Meanwhile, there was Jean Daddow's letter to be

considered. Sent to a journalist who had requested an interview, the letter was headed:

"TERRY AND JEAN LIFE STORY."

An accompanying note read:

"This is my story of my life as it really was and is. I hope this time the truth will be printed."

Describing her whirlwind romance with the bank manager and the elopement to Gretna Green, Jean Daddow related how the huge cash gift from the old woman had caused nasty rumours to circulate, and the woman's relatives to accuse the couple of fraud.

Writing of her affair with Terry Daddow, she said that once they got involved they tried to end the relationship because of the harm it might cause to their respective families. But it was too intense to end:

"There was such an incredible magnetism between us it was impossible. He would ring from the bank at work and at home. We started writing love letters. I wasn't much good at letters but Terry wrote beautiful poetry."

Then came the marriage, about which she said:

"My son thought we were mad because he had heard our stormy rows."

It was her second and his third attempt at matrimony. She complained that Terry Daddow was not easy to live with — he had a nasty temper.

She wrote:

"He was suffering an anxiety attack aggravated by alcohol. There were a few occasions when he was violent. A couple of times I called the police. But he was always sorry afterwards and I knew it was his illness that caused it. It was not the real Terry that I knew and loved."

This part of the letter was true. Her diary, later produced in court, recorded the details of her husband's violence. The entry for May 30th, 1991, read:

"Very bad. Me punch bag."

It was true that she had more than once had to run to neighbours for help. She was to claim that Terry liked to rape her, though there was no verification of this. But the police discovered that she often went to work at her hairdressing business in Tenterden with a bruised face.

Recalling the night of Terry's murder, Jean Daddow wrote:

"We had our drinking choc and then I went up to bed. While I was in the bedroom I heard a terrific bang. I listened, then came out of the bathroom and looked over the banisters."

She said she saw her husband lying crumpled at the foot of the stairs and went down to him.

"I could see Terry lying on the floor. His head was at the foot of the stairs. I sat on the stairs talking to him. I don't know how long I sat there for I thought his lips moved. Was he trying to say something? His dark eyes were looking at me. Blood was coming from his mouth.

"I did not know why Terry opened the door that night. I can only think the security light came on and he went to see if it was a badger. There have been many strange things said since my husband's death. Then on some woman's say-so of accusing her husband of killing Terry she said that I too and my son were involved.

"I am still in shock. No one knows how I really feel because I cannot put it in words. It is a feeling inside. Gutted. You never stop aching or shaking. I jump at every sound. I find it impossible to be on my own. I live in absolute fear of this gunman or woman. I'm nervous on my own and I'm only guilty of loving a sick husband."

The long letter was an attempt to plead her innocence, to protest that the police were intent on framing her for her husband's murder. But the evidence against her told a different story.

Bell had been the weak link in the murder plot. He had not been able to resist boasting of his skill, and a relative of his went to the police. In custody, Bell revealed the murder plot but denied having taken part in the killing, accusing Blackman of the shooting.

Jean Daddow, her son, and Bell appeared in the dock at Hove Crown Court on February 24th, 1993.

Mr. Richard Vanden Pratt QC, prosecuting, told the

jury that although Jean Daddow had said that she was horrified by the death of her husband, in fact she held a series of meetings with the killer to plot the deed, and those plots had taken place over a period of weeks. Robert Bell had confessed to the police that Mrs. Daddow and her son, Roger, had approached him about killing Terry Daddow.

As for the motive, the prosecutor claimed that Terry Daddow had treated his wife violently and she and her son had grown to hate him. Mr. Daddow had also threatened to sell up and move away, leaving Jean Daddow homeless and penniless ...

Robert Bell told the court of the murder plots, claiming he had deliberately bungled attempts to kill Terry Daddow. He had only agreed to take part in order to stall for time to raise the money to pay off his drugs debt, he said.

He described the first attempt, when at 3.30 a.m. on October 11th, 1991, Blackman drove him to Chapelfield Cottage on his motorcycle, giving Bell his motorcycle helmet to disguise his identity, along with a steel cosh. Jean Daddow had turned off the automatic security lighting around the house and left a door unlocked. She had also helpfully removed any floor ornaments that might impede Bell. He had taken only three steps into the house before fleeing when he heard Terry Daddow stirring in his bed.

On October 19th there was another attempt when Terry and Jean Daddow set off on a holiday trip to the West Country. Bell was ordered to follow them and kill Terry when an opportunity arose. Bell told the court, "Jean thought it would be an ideal place for Terry to be killed. She said I could mix with the tourists and also the hotel was very remote."

Although Bell went to Devon, he did not approach the hotel where the Daddows were staying. Instead, he went to a nearby town and purchased a 9 mm Browning blank-firing pistol, hoping to impress the murderous mother and son that he intended to carry out the killing now that he had a suitable weapon. He did not tell them it was a replica which only fired blanks . . .

In the course of the following month Jean and her son suggested a number of ways in which Bell should kill Terry. He could shoot him from a car when he went out shopping. Terry liked going out walking near Dungeness. Bell was told to hide behind a rock and shoot Terry as he passed. Again the attempt was botched.

One morning Jean informed Bell that she was going to drive Terry over to her parents' house, where she would have to park off the road. She instructed Bell to come roaring round the corner in his car and run Terry down as he crossed the road. Bell said he refused, saying it was too dangerous with too many witnesses about.

Poison was the next strategy. Bell was to turn up at Chapelfield Cottage on November 10th, 1991, and pretend to be a conservation officer with expertise in badgers. Terry was furious about badgers digging up his garden and had fought a long and futile battle against them. At the house, Bell passed an envelope, given to him by Blackman, to Jean Daddow. It contained a mixture of ectasy tablets and amphetamine sulphate; enough, it was thought, to kill Terry outright. The wife duly gave this to her husband in a drink, but it only made him very ill. The next day he wrote to his doctor saying he feared he was going completely mad as he was hallucinating and seeing wild geese.

On leaving the cottage, Bell visited several neighbours to talk about badgers, in order to make his story believable. All of those neighbours were able to describe Bell to the police following the murder.

Three days before the shooting Bell offered to make a bomb to do the job. He said he used an empty Walkman case which he filled with Plasticine to make it look like Semtex. He then wrapped it in silver tape and left a few electric wires sticking out. He told the mother and son that it was a remote-control bomb, and taped it to the chassis of the Daddow family car.

"Jean was more than ready to go along with this," Bell told the jury. "She had said on more than one occasion that she didn't mind losing a car over this."

Then Bell told the mother and son that there would be a delay before he could obtain the remote-control device to detonate the explosive. So for a few days Jean Daddow drove around with what she thought was a bomb attached to her car.

Jean Daddow had been aware of the testimony Bell was going to give. She had passed copies of his statement to the police. Now all she could do was to go into the witness box and vehemently deny everything that Bell had said, dismissing it as a pack of lies. She said Bell was "obviously a nutter."

She even tried to blacken her husband's character in court, saying that he had told her that he had dreamed up a scheme for blackmailing old women with sexually explicit photographs taken after he had drugged their drinks. She claimed ignorance of her husband's deals, and denied knowledge of any plot to kill him. For all his deceits, she was devoted to him, she said.

On April 8th, 1993, all the defendants were found guilty. Jean Daddow and her son, Roger Blackman, were convicted of conspiring to commit murder, and Robert Bell was found guilty of murder. Neither mother nor son showed any emotion when the verdicts were announced, but Bell shook his head in disbelief.

Trial judge Mr. Justice Hidden then adjourned sentencing for three weeks.

Right to the end of her seven week trial, Jean Daddow had continued to play the heartbroken widow, telling reporters that she still carried a wedding photograph of Terry, and protesting, "I am not the callous person they are making me out to be."

On May 19th, 1993, Mr. Justice Hidden jailed Robert Bell for life with a recommendation that he should serve a minimum of 15 years and gave him a concurrent 18-year sentence for conspiracy to murder. Jean Daddow and Roger Blackman were both jailed for 18 years for conspiracy to murder.

A mother and her son are involved in a case from America that must rank as one of the strangest in the history of murder.

11
MOTHER LOVE

David Drew

**"I believe her. My mother holds
her mouth in a certain way when
she lies ..."**

BECAUSE Detective Lieutenant Charles R. Thompson of the Santa Barbara Police Department was under two weeks suspension for calling a superior officer what a superior officer never should be called he almost missed investigating the most macabre case the city ever encountered.

He was at home, cooling his heels and his head on the morning of November 18th, 1958, when pretty, blonde Mrs. Adeline Curry reached the apartment of 29-year-old Mrs. Olga Kupczyk Duncan, at 114 Garden Street. Olga, a nurse in the city's St. Francis Hospital, was to have assisted in an operation that morning. She'd failed to appear, and the hospital had telephoned her home. Receiving no reply, the head nurse sent Olga's closest friend, Nurse Curry, to investigate.

Mrs. Curry found the apartment's sliding glass door wide open, the lights on, but Olga nowhere around. Knowing that her colleague was six months pregnant, the worried Adeline telephone Olga's husband, attorney Frank Patrick Duncan, Jr., at his office. He in turn called the police.

Captain A. C. Wade, chief of detectives, sent an officer to investigate.

The Duncan apartment was shipshape. There was no evidence of forced entry, no sign of a struggle. The bed had been turned down as though the occupant was about to retire. The clothing Olga must have worn the previous evening lay on a chair; green slippers underneath it. One thing particularly suggested that Mrs. Duncan had not planned her departure. Her handbag stood on a table. It contained money and cosmetics. Had Olga intended to leave she would surely have taken these essentials.

Two other nurses had visited Olga the night before. They had left around 11 p.m., when the pregnant woman was about to go to bed. Mrs. Duncan had mentioned no trip, and had seemed to be in good spirits.

Her lawyer husband did not live at the Garden Street address, but instead stayed with his 54-year-old mother, Mrs. Elizabeth Duncan, in the La Morada Apartments in Santa Barbara. When the officer called on him the worried attorney described his missing wife as very pretty, with brown hair and blue eyes. Born in Vancouver, British Columbia, she had come to Santa Barbara a year earlier. They had been married in June, 1958, but separated in August, Olga taking the Garden Street flat, Duncan returning to his mother.

"When did you last see your wife?" he was asked.

About 10 days earlier, on his birthday, November 7th, he had spent the evening in her apartment, leaving at about 1.30 a.m. They remained on good terms despite the separation. In fact, Duncan told the detective, "I'm still very much in love with Olga. I hoped some day we might work things out and get together again."

The detective tactfully inquired whether Olga might have a boy friend. Duncan snorted disbelief. His mother was equally incredulous. Olga had her faults, but she was no gadabout. Mother and son urged the police to make further inquiries. If Olga was in trouble, they wanted to help.

A missing-person report was filed, neighbours were interviewed, and there matters stood when Lieutenant Thompson returned to duty.

His findings convinced his superiors that this was no routine missing-person case, and it was at this point that Chief of Detectives Wade received a call from a man who said Olga was not married to Frank Duncan at the time she disappeared.

"What!"

"Yes. The marriage was annulled in Ventura Superior Court on August 7th, 1958."

That was just at the time the couple separated. Captain Wade summoned Duncan.

"Why didn't you tell me that you had had your marriage annulled?"

Frank's mouth gaped. "Annulled!" he shouted. "What on earth do you mean?"

"Your marriage was annulled in Ventura on August 7th!"

Duncan shook his head vigorously. "I don't know what you're talking about! I wasn't in Ventura in August! Olga and I instituted no proceedings! I was right here in Santa Barbara on August seventh, and not thirty miles away in Ventura!"

Officers drove to Ventura and examined the record. Yes, Olga and Frank Duncan had indubitably gone through annulment proceedings, claiming that the marriage was never consummated. Yet Duncan admitted seeing his wife after that. And she was pregnant!

Photostats of the documents were brought to Santa Barbara. The signature of Olga Duncan on the annulment papers did not match her signature on records at the hospital!

So who was the Olga Duncan who had appeared in the Ventura court? And the signature of Frank Duncan on the annulment papers did not match the signature of the known Frank Duncan, as it appeared on official documents in Santa Barbara! So who was the Frank Duncan who had had his marriage to Olga Duncan erased?

Questioned by Thompson, Ventura's Hal Hammons, Jr., the attorney of record in the annulment matter, confirmed his part in the proceedings. And Hammons added that about three weeks later he had had occasion to telephone Duncan about it. Duncan was nonplussed, and said he didn't know what Hammons was talking about.

Now, Hammons said, he had discovered he'd been tricked. The people who had come to him were not Olga and Frank Duncan.

"We know that," Captain Wade told him. "But who *did* get the annulment?"

"Well, I can identify 'Olga.' "

"You can?"

"Yes. It was Mrs. Elizabeth Duncan, the mother of Frank Duncan."

Hammons said he had been surprised by Frank Duncan's reaction on the phone when called about the annulment. Then he received a call from a Santa Barbara attorney. Elizabeth Duncan had called on him, saying that she and someone she'd hired had impersonated Olga and Frank and gained the annulment. Mrs. Duncan wanted the Santa Barbara lawyer to break the news to her son. Shocked, he had refused the assignment. She then asked him to drop the matter. Instead, concerned about the ethics of withholding such information, the attorney telephoned Hammons, who now relayed all he knew to Captain Wade.

Lieutenant Thompson discovered that Mrs. Elizabeth Duncan had opposed the marriage of Olga and her son. Many people had told him so, Nurse Curry alerting him to the intensity of the opposition. The irony was that Frank had met Olga when she was ministering to his mother, who had been rushed to the hospital after taking an overdose of sleeping pills.

Why the overdose? She'd quarrelled with her son when he'd announced he wanted to take quarters of his own.

Mrs. Duncan wouldn't accept the idea of her son leaving her. She was all the more in a tizzy when the love affair blossomed between Frank and Olga. And she was devastated by the marriage, which took place without her knowledge.

Nurse Curry told Thompson that Olga had confided that she had been abused by Elizabeth Duncan after the marriage. Mother Duncan wasn't going to give up her boy! She'd see Olga in hell first!

Another witness said that Olga had told her that when Frank had brought her home after the wedding, she'd slept in a room by herself while Frank and his mother shared an adjoining one.

That was the picture the detective lieutenant unveiled. Shortly after the bogus annulment was uncovered the Santa Barbara officials received word from Olga's father in Canada. His daughter had written many letters home complaining of her mother-in-law. These were forwarded. One indicated that whenever Frank was out of the house Mrs. Elizabeth Duncan showed up to revile her daughter-in-law.

"All is not well with Frank and me," Olga had written to her mother. "Frank's mother has lived with Frank for so long that she has an uncanny hold on him. She is a very possessive woman, and has not allowed him out of her sight. Therefore Frank is not really grown up. He's never been away from home."

Mrs. Duncan, the letter related, phoned a dozen times a day to curse Olga. "She went all around the neighbourhood ... saying I was already married ... that I had two children ... She cut up Frank's baptismal certificate and all his baby pictures ... She has not allowed Frank to live here. He has a great problem ..."

Too great a problem. Frank Patrick Duncan Jr. left Olga and returned home to his mother.

The two were deeply attached. Court employees privately dubbed Frank "mama's boy." He often entered the courtroom hand in hand with his mother. She would sit up front, eyes alight with love as her son addressed the bench.

Studying his earlier notes it occurred to Lieutenant Thompson that one of Mrs. Elizabeth Duncan's neighbours, an elderly woman, Mrs. Emma B. Short, had never been interviewed alone. Mrs. Duncan was always hovering about her. He wondered why.

He employed a ruse that drew Mrs. Duncan out of the house. Then he called on Emma Short, who was delighted and relieved. She had a lot she wanted to tell the officer but hadn't dared to in Elizabeth's presence — and Elizabeth was not letting her out of her sight these days.

Mrs. Short told Thompson that she knew about the annulment. Moreover, she gave a description of Frank's stand-in in the phoney affair. She had seen the man the day that he and Mrs. Elizabeth Duncan set off for Ventura. She knew him only as Ralph. He had mentioned working in a Santa Barbara café, and groused about having to support his children.

The witness added that Mrs. Duncan once planned to have Olga kidnapped! The elderly neighbour overheard a conversation between Elizabeth and an unidentified man along those lines. A Mrs. Esperanza Esquivel figured in the conversation.

Her story told, Mrs. Short pleaded for police protection and was whisked off to a hiding-place.

The police checked all the Ralphs in the failure-to-provide files, and came up with a Ralph William Winterstein. Mrs. Short identified him as Frank Duncan's stand-in.

Lieutenant Thompson next called on Mrs. Esperanza Esquivel. She was well known in Santa Barbara as proprietor of the Tropical Restaurant, and with her husband, Marcano, had been a client of Frank Duncan Jr.

She said that Mrs. Duncan had called on her, asking if she could get a couple of men to do a job.

Mrs. Esquivel asked a couple of nice fellows who hung out at the Tropical whether they were interested in earning some money. They were. She introduced them to Mrs. Duncan, but she didn't know what type of work Mrs. Duncan had in mind.

A job meant money. Lieutenant Thompson found that four days before Olga disappeared Elizabeth had withdrawn $200 from her son's account without his knowledge. The next day she pawned some jewellery for $175.

On December 15th, 1958 — one month after Olga Duncan disappeared — the Santa Barbara police announced that Mrs. Elizabeth Duncan was being held, along with Augustine Baldonado, 25, and Luis Moya, 22, in the matter of her missing daughter-in-law. Baldonado was being booked on suspicion of kidnapping. Moya was charged only with parole violation — driving a car without his parole officer's permission.

What did Mrs. Elizabeth Duncan say when arrested, reporters wanted to know. First, she entered a general denial. Then she admitted that she had posed as Olga, and secured an annulment to her son's marriage. She didn't know the name of the man who had posed as Frank, she insisted.

"It was as if she'd picked him up off the street," said District Attorney Roy A. Gustafson, shaking his head.

Elizabeth flatly denied planning a kidnapping, denied knowing Baldonado or Moya, and insisted she had no idea of the whereabouts of her daughter-in-law.

Baldonado said he'd never been approached by Mrs. Duncan, and has done no job for her. Moya said the same.

And Frank Duncan Jr.? He was right beside his mother, as her counsel, clear of suspicion himself, shocked, bewildered, but firmly convinced that she was innocent. He could not and would not believe that the woman who had nurtured him, put him through law school and attended to his every need could be guilty of anything as frightful as was being hinted at by the papers.

Before Olga's disappearance the police had stopped a 1948 Chevrolet going through a red light. The driver was James Roja, 19. Lieutenant Thompson now remembered that there were three passengers and that Luis Moya was one.

He checked back, Roja had been jailed on a number of traffic charges and was in prison. Meanwhile the police had spotted the Chevvy again, this time with improper licence plates. It was found that the car belonged to a Pedro Contreras. But he too was in jail. He'd been there since before Olga's disappearance.

Thompson called on Contreras's wife, Sara. She knew both Moya and Baldonado. A generous girl, she had loaned the car to Roja. She had also made it available to Baldonado and Moya just about the time that Olga disappeared. They'd offered her $25 for rental of the vehicle. That was almost more than the car was worth, so Sara agreed. They returned it with the upholstery in the back all cut and pulled apart, explaining that a cigarette had ignited the fabric and they had been forced to cut it away.

Sara had settled for $10 damages. She was sure the trip the boys had taken was innocent. Kidnap? She shrugged. "How was I to know about anything like that? Gus and Luis are just a couple of fun-loving guys, real crazy. They like to dance, they like to drink. Everybody likes them."

The Chevvy was now examined, and human blood was found on the padding underneath the ripped-away upholstery . . .

On December 18th Mrs. Elizabeth Duncan, fashionably dressed and smiling, appeared in court for arraignment and a plea for reduction of bail.

Her son thundered, "I believe, bluntly, that this is the time for the authorities to put up or shut up! They are holding my mother on $50,000 bail, which is completely unreasonable."

If, he claimed, the authorities had any real charges to bring, they had had plenty of time to file them.

Bail was reduced to $5,000. That might be put up in a matter of hours. The authorities would indeed have to put up or shut up.

"We intend to put up!" Gustafson growled.

After court Frank Duncan informed the press that his mother had never told him that she had obtained a false annulment because she realised the seriousness of what she had done. "I was the last one she wanted to know about it. I wanted no divorce. I wanted no annulment. I wanted to live with Olga."

He was asked if he thought his wife was alive. He replied that that was his hope.

"Was your mother trying to break up your marriage?"

Duncan wet his lips. "Well, she ... uh ... let's say she hindered its development."

"Did you ever ask your mother whether she knew anything about your wife's disappearance?"

"Many times," Frank nodded. "Before she was arrested, and since then. Believe me, I am a good cross-examiner, and I gave her the most rigorous cross-examination possible. She broke down. She cried. But she told me, positively and absolutely, that she had nothing to do with it."

"You believe that?" a reporter asked.

"I believe her. My mother holds her mouth in a certain way when she lies, and she wasn't lying when I questioned her."

Meanwhile at headquarters Augustin Baldonado and Luis Moya were being relentlessly interrogated. An alert went out for Ralph William Winterstein, Frank Duncan's stand-in, who was probably on some skidrow, having long since gurgled down the $60 that Mrs. Duncan had paid him for his services in the bogus marriage annulment.

And James Roja, in jail, remembered that he had lent Baldonado a .22 calibre revolver in good working condition on November 15th. When it was returned on November 22nd it was broken. How had it been used?

Mrs. Esquivel, pressed further, recalled that Elizabeth Duncan had promised $6,000 for the job of doing something to somebody.

The day Olga was found to be missing, Baldonado and

Moya had shown up at Mrs. Esquivel's café in blood-stained clothes, to change. Moya said, "We have done Mrs. Duncan's job." Baldonado added. "They'll never find the witch. The body is behind a pipe. I had to hit the witch. She sure did scream!"

All that work for a pittance! Mrs. Esquivel heard that Mrs. Duncan had come through with a paltry $600, not $6,000.

A massive hunt was launched for the body of Olga Duncan. Wherever there were pipes there were men searching. Meanwhile the police announced that Mrs. Elizabeth Duncan was no stranger to marriage annulments. The last three of her seven marriages had ended in annulment, and her husbands had included men more than 20 years her junior — one of them a fellow-student of her son at law school.

In 1953 she had been arrested for running a massage parlour as a front for prostitution.

To prevent the springing of the prisoner, District Attorney Gustafson lodged an additional charge against Mrs. Duncan: conspiracy to kidnap and murder Olga Duncan. Bail was set at $100,000.

As officers combed the countryside Police Chief R. W. Cooley broadcast an appeal for anyone with information to come forward. Olga's body was disposed of between 12.30 a.m. and 5 a.m., he said. "It was placed — you will note I don't say buried; I am not sure of that — beside or under a pipe. This pipe may have been loose, and it was located near a post of some kind.

"The pipe is somewhere near a road, and at the time the body was being disposed of, another car drove by.

"There was poison oak in the immediate area where the body was left ..."

The police knew that the car had been in use for about five hours. The kidnappers could have driven a maximum of $2\frac{1}{2}$ hours each way. The pipe — perhaps a sewer construction ditch — was somewhere within that driving distance.

The hunt could be narrowed down by the poison oak clue. Officers had noted poison oak spores on the two male suspects, believed to have been contracted while depositing the body.

On December 21st Cecil Lambert telephoned headquarters. He had seen two men before dawn on November 18th, emerging from a ditch as he'd driven by the Casistas Dam area.

While officers went to the scene Detective Ray Higgins tried to get Baldonado to confess.

Higgins chatted about the prisoner's wife and children. He asked about Baldonado's twin sons, born a month before. He sent for sandwiches. For an hour he just chatted. He showed the prisoner a paper — perhaps Baldonado wanted to read the comics. It so happened that the front page was full of news about the Duncan case, revealing how much the police already had in the way of evidence.

Baldonado gulped and turned to the comic section. Higgins let him finish it and then increased the pressure. Where did Baldonado say he had been after midnight and in the early morning of November 18th?

How were Baldonado's folks taking all this? Nice family! Was that his sister, the fine-looking girl who brought him cigarettes? Too bad they all had to go through this!

It would get worse, too. Had he noticed all that the police now knew? Right there, in the paper. Why didn't Baldonado get it over with, spare himself and the family a lot more grief? What was done was done, he'd have to pay for it, it would be plenty bad; but why must his whole family suffer?

Suddenly Baldonado threw up his hands and said, "O.K.! I'll tell you everything for nobody except my people; the kids!"

He and Moya had met Mrs. Elizabeth Duncan twice at the Tropical Restaurant, the first time on November 12th. On the 14th the figure of $6,000 for the job was agreed upon. On November 17th the two young men drove to

Garden Street. Moya went in to lure Olga out by saying that her husband was drunk, sick and requiring attention in the car outside.

Olga emerged in nightgown and robe. She bent over the man in the back seat, thinking it was Frank Duncan. But it was Baldonado. He knocked her out with the gun and threw her into the car. He drove while Moya struggled with the woman on the back seat as she regained consciousness. He choked and struck her, but she wouldn't die.

At a road-fill project near the Casistas Dam which the kidnappers had spotted the day before, Baldonado stopped, scrambled down the ravine and scratched at the earth to form a grave.

He returned to the car. Olga was still fighting. Baldonado grabbed the gun and battered her head until she lay still. He wasn't such a cruel guy, Baldonado told Detective Higgins. He'd planned to shoot Olga, the humane way, but that knucklehead Moya had ruined the gun by his inept bludgeoning.

To make sure that the job was done according to what the lady with the $6,000 wanted, each man now took turns strangling Olga. Then they threw her into the hole, pitched a little dirt over her and departed.

Baldonado finished his confession, wiped the sweat from his face and whispered, "I want to see a priest!"

Word was flashed to the detectives in the field. Baldonado was brought out to lead the party to the grave. He went unerringly to the place. It exactly fitted the description given in Police Chief Cooley's broadcast appeal: there was the pipe, the nearby post and the poison oak. And there in the shallow grave lay the body, on its side, knees drawn up like a baby's.

The coroner thought it possible that Olga had been interred before she was dead. "I don't know!" Baldonado protested. "We strangled her, and I *think* we killed her before we put her in the hole."

After the body was returned the seven miles to Santa

Barbara, Luis Moya was told that Baldonado had confessed and implicated him. Moya put his hand to his head, moaning, "How could he say that? Believe me! Believe me! I didn't have nothin' to do with it!"

Told about the confession, Elizabeth Duncan said with a smile, "It's a lie, of course."

A reporter asked why she had given Baldonado and Moya money if they had done nothing for her. "I never gave them money for anything like *that*!" she exclaimed. "They were blackmailing me, of course." She had been told, Mrs. Duncan said, that her son would come to harm unless she paid up.

Meanwhile Frank Duncan Jr. disappeared. A news flash carrying word that the body of his wife had been found was broadcast at 2 a.m. At 3 a.m. he left his house, carrying luggage.

Gustafson announced that he wanted him as a witness, and if he didn't show up an alert would go out for him.

At this point attorney S. Ward Sullivan announced that Frank Duncan Jr. had retained him to represent his mother.

On Christmas Day, Luis Moya broke. He confessed that he had told Olga her husband was in the car, drunk and passed-out. Frank had a lot of money on him. Would his wife help him into the apartment? And Olga had walked out into a death trap.

On December 26th Frank Duncan Jr. was located in Hollywood, living under an assumed name in an apartment on which he had paid two months' rent in advance. Told that his mother and the two self-confessed slayers were about to be indicted for murder, he exclaimed, "This charge is preposterous! I never recall my mother doing anything violent. She is incapable of physical cruelty or violence. My mother would have had to be insane to do anything like this."

Mrs. Short, however, not only told of the kidnap plans but also swore that she had been asked to aid in a scheme in which Elizabeth Duncan would be the executioner.

The witness said, "She (Mrs. Duncan) asked me to go over to her (Olga's) apartment and ... to try to get her to come over to my apartment. When I got her to my apartment I would have her sit in a chair that is against my closet. Mrs. Duncan would be in the closet. She would take a rope and put it around her (Olga's) neck and choke her. She would throw this poison in her eyes."

Frank Patricia Duncan Jr. took the stand. He insisted that he and his mother enjoyed a normal relationship. However, he conceded, she did dominate him, even to the point of forbidding him to live with his wife.

Next to testify was Olga's landlady. She told of the time that Elizabeth Duncan had called on her daughter-in-law and found her absent. "She flew right to the bedroom and she took me by surprise ... She flung open the closet door and started screaming, 'There, you see! You see! None of his clothes are here! Look at that bed! There is only one pillow! They are not married!'

"And she continued screaming, 'I told you they are not married! They are not married, and she has taken him away from me!'

"Well, of course, while she was talking about all this I got a little irate, and I said, 'How old is your son?' She said, 'Twenty-nine,' and I said, 'What is he? A man or mouse?' I said, 'If I told one of my sons whom he should live with, he would kick me out and I would deserve it.'

A pretty carhop at the Blue Onion drive-in restaurant took the stand. The café was across the street from the apartment where Mrs. Duncan lived. Early in August 1958 Elizabeth approached her. "She wanted me to go to the house and take care of Olga. And I asked her what she meant, and she said she had plenty of acid and anything else that was needed. She asked me if I would go to the door and ring the doorbell. And when the girl answered the door, throw the acid in her face ... that she (Mrs. Duncan) would be behind me and take a blanket and put over the girl and drag her out to the car and drive her up to the mountains and push her over a cliff ... If I had only told the right person then, Olga would be alive today."

Frank Duncan now told reporters, "I don't know — I just don't know. Mother would have to be insane to have done a thing like that. The jury will have to decide."

Elizabeth Duncan claimed that Baldonado and Moya, inspired by Mrs. Esquivel, had persecuted and extorted money from her because Frank hadn't saved Marcano Esquivel from prison — and that they had finally killed her daughter-in-law in order to frame her (Elizabeth) for murder.

Arraigned in court on January 6th, 1959, she entered a double plea of not guilty and not guilty by reason of insanity.

On January 13th Baldonado and Moya entered the same double plea, and the trial of the trio began on February 16th. A month later they were found guilty of first-degree murder, and on March 25th after studying psychiatric reports, Judge Charles Blackstock ruled Elizabeth Duncan sane and all three were sentenced to die in the gas chamber.

The murder trio were executed in San Quentin on August 8th, 1962. Moya and Baldonado died together. Elizabeth died alone . . .

THE KIDNAP GAME

12
THE BADGER GAME

William Kendal

"And they call women the weaker sex"

"POP" KENT loved female company. Although 73, he still had an eye for a pretty woman. To many, however, he was a bit of a mystery. William Kent did no work, yet he never seemed short of money — it was not unusual to see him buy a round of drinks from a fat wad of notes.

True, he owned the house in which he occupied a ground-floor room, letting out the rest to boarders. But the shabby building in the run-down Melbourne suburb of Carlton had only two storeys, and there were not enough tenants to bring in much money.

The boarders all knew that what they paid Pop each week couldn't finance his free-spending. They also knew he had another source of income. He was an off-track bookie, conducting his business on the streets and at the nearby University Hotel.

One of his tenants was Jim Conole, who shared the upstairs front room with his wife. In the early evening of Tuesday, November 8th, 1949, he saw Pop drinking with a sexy redhead at the University Hotel, and he guessed the woman's next destination would be the landlord's room. Fancying the cheap thrill of a second look at her, at about 6.30 Conole went down to Kent's room on the pretext of borrowing a newspaper, and popped his head round the door.

Sure enough, the redhead was there — sitting on Pop Kent's lap. But the couple were not alone. Two men who had been with the woman in the pub were also in Pop's room. Having run his eye appreciatively over the redhead's shapely legs and no less attractive bust, Conole thanked Pop for the paper and left to keep a drinking appointment with some pals in the suburb of Hawthorn.

Ninety minutes later May Howard became disturbed by the noises coming from Pop's room next door. Although the dividing wall was thick, she fancied she could hear someone moving furniture. She also thought she detected thuds and groans.

She knew Pop had company — around 6 p.m. she had seen him come home with a red-headed woman and two men. She had later seen the woman and one of the men come out into the hallway, lock Kent's door, pocket the key and go out to the back yard, where she heard them talking. Then they returned and let themselves back into Pop's room.

Something else unusual had happened that evening. Most nights Mrs. McWilliam from across the street would come over for a drink with Pop Kent. She was always made welcome, but tonight was an exception. May Howard heard her voice raised in protest, saying her husband knew where she was and she visited Pop "regular." But it seemed she had been given short shrift, for moments later Mrs. Howard saw her return to her home.

As nine o'clock approached May realised that Pop's room was now quiet. Although the earlier noises had worried her, she found the silence even more unnerving.

She knocked on Pop's door. There was no response. She turned the knob, but the door was locked. That was strange. Pop never usually locked his door when he was in, so perhaps he'd gone out again with his visitors. Or perhaps ...

May Howard knew she'd get no sleep that night unless she made sure Pop was all right. Maybe he'd gone out with his visitors. She put her ear to the keyhole and listened. Someone was still there. She could faintly hear voices.

She had earlier expressed her uneasiness to another tenant, elderly William Symons, who had lost a leg in the First World War. She went back to his room, telling him she was still worried and was going outside to have a peep through Pop's window.

To do this she took a discreet, circuitous route, leaving by the back yard and going round the block until she was near Mrs. McWilliam's home on the other side of the street. She stood there a few minutes, looking across at Pop's window. Through the open front door she saw one of the two men in the hallway. A moment later he was joined by the other man and the redhead, the second man calling out "Goodnight" as he closed the landlord's door behind him.

Outside on the pavement the trio chatted briefly and then strolled off together, vanishing around the street corner. Mrs. Howard went back to Symons's room and reported their departure. Symons asked if she had heard Pop reply when one of the visitors wished him goodnight. May said she hadn't.

The pair went to Pop's door. Symons knocked, to be greeted only by silence. He gave a louder knock, this time with one of his crutches. There was still no response. May wanted to break in, but Symons said that was a job for the police, so she hurried out to the nearest call-box to phone them.

Detective Constable George Crouch and two uniformed officers were the first to arrive. They forced Pop Kent's door open, took one look at the ransacked room and the body on the floor, and called headquarters for homicide detectives. Senior Detective Cyril Currer and Detective Constable Ron Kellett were among the first to respond, stepping gingerly around the debris of the room where a few hours earlier William Kent had cuddled the red-headed woman on his knee.

Now he lay on his left side, partly covered by a blood-spattered sheet, his face bruised and battered almost beyond recognition. The carpet around him had been slashed and pulled apart in several places, exposing the floorboards; the mattress on his bed had been slit, its stuffing spilling onto the floor; the wardrobe lay on its side, its panels knocked out; the dressing-table was also overturned, its drawers and their contents scattered. It didn't need a detective to see that somebody had been looking for something.

But a doctor was required to examine the body before it was disturbed, and pathologist Dr. Keith Bowden was soon on hand. The sheet was pulled back to reveal the elderly victim's shirt, ripped open to expose his blood-stained torso. He had cuts in his throat, his upper lip and under his left eye; his nose had been all but pulped and there were what appeared to be fingernail scratches on his neck and cigarette burns on his chest. More injuries were to be revealed before the examination finished. The doctor said the victim had apparently been tortured before he died.

Pop Kent's wrists had been bound behind him with a strip torn from a sheet, his thumbs had been tied together with a bootlace and his pockets were inside-out. The police had been aware of his illicit bookmaking, but had never succeeded in nailing him. Told of the old man's three visitors, the investigators surmised that the girl had acted as bait, talking the victim into inviting her and her companions home for drinks, with suggestions of a bit of sex on the side. It was speculated that on learning of Kent's occupation the trio had decided he must have cash stashed in his room. Failing to find it, they had murdered him to prevent him identifying them, or perhaps just out of rage.

Jim Conole arrived home at 11 p.m. while the detectives were speculating. He told them not only what he'd seen but also what he'd heard. One of the men, he said, had addressed the redhead as "Jean." The four had been sharing a bottle of wine in Pop's room, and "Jean" had been a bit of all right ... except for her nose. She had a sore on it which she kept scratching.

Officers were sent to the University Hotel to hear what the staff could recall of Pop's three companions. The investigators already had good descriptions of them from Mrs. Howard, Conole and several other neighbours.

The barman remembered the redhead distinctly — right down to the sore on her nose. She'd been playing-up to Pop Kent, he said, and he'd heard her say that she and her companions were from Sydney.

Airports and railway stations were checked for reports of the trio leaving town, but that line of inquiry drew a blank, as the investigators expected. It was the week of the Melbourne Cup, Australia's premier horse race. That was what had probably brought the three suspects to the city. The detectives believed they'd be staying on in the hope of backing a winner with their loot. So the next step was to check all the hotels.

At the Great Southern Hotel near the Spencer Street railway terminal the night receptionist was more than helpful. He said the trio's descriptions resembled three guests who had arrived the previous day. A Mr. Andrews had taken a single room, and his companions Mr. and Mrs. Lee had taken a double.

Senior Detective William Mooney was given the suspects' room-keys. A bloodstained coat and skirt lay in the bottom of the Lees' wardrobe, together with a shirt with blood on the cuffs; and in Andrews's room a blood-spattered shirt was draped on a chair.

Mooney and the three detectives accompanying him returned to the hotel's lobby and phoned headquarters, asking Currer and Kellett to join them. Then the four settled down inconspicuously in the lobby to await the return of their quarry.

It had been a long day, and some of them dozed off. But just before 4.20 a.m. the sound of laughter startled them awake. Two male hotel guests had entered the lobby. Like the red-headed woman with them, they were drunk, and they were joking with the night porter. The redhead had a red sore on her nose.

As the four detectives moved in to surround the trio they were joined by Currer and Kellett. The three suspects were asked politely to accompany the officers to headquarters "to assist them with their inquiries." But first, the redhead was asked to turn out her handbag. Its contents included two airline tickets in the names of Mr. and Mrs. Clayton. There were protests, but the trio then went quietly in separate cars. Little more than seven hours had elapsed since Mrs. Howard made her phone call to the police.

At headquarters the three suspects were placed in separate rooms. Mooney and a colleague questioned "Mr. Lee," who now identified himself as Robert Clayton. He said the redhead was his girl friend Jean Lee. The detectives sensed that she was a prostitute and that Clayton — a mean-looking small man — was her lover and pimp.

He said they had met Norman Andrews earlier in the week, and ever since the three had gone around together. During the previous afternoon Andrews had pawned a suit because they were short of money. They had subsequently got into conversation with an elderly man addressed as "Pop" in the lounge at the University Hotel.

Jean and Andrews had accompanied Pop home, Clayton continued, and he himself had waited for them outside the hotel.

That couldn't be true, Mooney told him: he had been seen walking with his companions and Pop to the old man's home in Dorrit Street.

"I was never there," Clayton insisted.

Mooney turned to the trio's finances. Andrews had received only £5 for his pawned suit, yet he still had £3 when arrested after an afternoon's drinking. And Clayton had £25. That hardly squared with Clayton's claim that they were short of cash.

Clayton said the £25 was money he'd saved from doing casual work in Sydney.

The interrogation continued, Mooney telling the suspect that his story didn't add up. He'd been seen going to Pop Kent's home. Furthermore, he'd been seen leaving there at about nine. The old man had been brutally murdered and robbed, and now Clayton and his companions, hard-up earlier in the day, were suddenly flush with money ... Pop's money.

Clayton continued to deny everything, but as the questioning continued he began to appreciate the implausibility of his story. "I'm not taking the rap for what the others did," he suddenly exploded.

He went on to claim that Jean and Andrews had wanted him to take part in snuffing Pop Kent, but he had refused. Jean had come out into Kent's back yard, he said, telling him that Pop had a thick wad of notes but his trousers were too tight across his stomach for her to get it "the sweet way." So the victim would have to be done over.

Clayton said that after returning briefly to Pop's room he had gone back to the Great Southern Hotel, leaving Jean and Andrews to get on with it and meeting up with them later.

Asked where the trio had got the money for their airline tickets to Adelaide, Clayton said Andrews and Jean had got it when they robbed their victim.

Mooney reminded him that he had been seen leaving Pop's home with the other two, and that abrasions on his hands showed he had been using his fists. Told that he was being charged with Kent's murder, Clayton dictated a statement repeating what he had said in the interview, and then signed it.

Mooney moved on to Jean Lee, who was being questioned by Currer and Kellett. Currer joined Mooney outside the room, telling him that the suspect was keeping her cool and admitting nothing.

Mooney went back into the room and told her of

Clayton's account of her conversation with him in Pop Kent's back yard. She repeated that she was saying nothing. Mooney then told her that Clayton had signed a statement. She asked to see it, and the detective fetched it and read it to her. She accused the detectives of making it up and asked to see Clayton. When they brought him in to her he burst into tears. She looked at him with contempt, still refusing to talk.

But there were tears in her eyes too after Clayton was escorted away. "And they call women the weaker sex!" she said. "Well, I love Bobby, the poor sod. And I always will. If that's the way he wants it, he can have it."

She told the detectives that Clayton was telling the truth up to the point where he said he left Kent's house. He had not left by himself. Andrews had gone with him, leaving her alone with Pop.

"I hit him with a bottle and a piece of wood," she continued. The detectives had noted a broken chair-leg found beside the body. "I cut my finger on the bottle." She held out her hand to display the injury. "He fell over in the chair. Then he fell on the floor."

Asked if she had tied the victim's hands, she said: "Yes, I tied his thumbs with a bit of cord. I knew he was dead when we left him."

"We?" asked Currer.

"There was only me," she insisted.

Invited to put that in writing, she declined, reverting to denying everything and refusing to say any more. She too was charged with the old man's murder.

Andrews, like Clayton, denied going to Pop Kent's home. The other two might have "been in it," he said, but he wasn't with them.

Told of Clayton's statement, he expressed disbelief, demanding to see it. Having done so, he was enraged. "Okay, so I was there," he admitted. "But I didn't do him. I never even hit him." He said that Clayton and Jean had attacked and robbed the victim, while he himself just stood by.

His attention was directed to his skinned knuckles. They didn't look like those of someone who had just stood and watched. Told that he was being charged with murder, he protested, "I didn't touch him."

As the three suspects awaited trial the police took stock of their backgrounds. Jean Lee had been a bright school pupil with an inquiring mind; a bit of a tomboy and inclined to be rebellious. Head-turningly pretty as a teenager, she had drifted from one job to another, giving none of her employers satisfaction. As a milliner's assistant, a waitress, a garage clerk and a factory worker she had seemed more interested in young men than her job.

Her marriage at 18 to a feckless long-time boy friend had been followed by the birth of a daughter. The marriage didn't work out, she filed for divorce and her mother took over the care of the child.

Moving to Brisbane in 1942, Jean got another job as a waitress, dated American servicemen and became the lover of a petty crook who was to dominate the next four years of her life. He introduced her to prostitution and became her pimp. In 1946 she broke away from him and became a Sydney barmaid, also working in a brothel.

Then she met Robert Clayton, the petty criminal who was to control the rest of her life. A housebreaker and conman, he was three years older than Jean, who fell deeply in love with him despite his shifty, runtish appearance.

She had taken to drink — which she couldn't handle — and he quickly became her minder, the two becoming accomplished exponents of "the badger game." This required Jean to select a well-heeled, respectable-looking male, lure him to her stolen car, expose her breasts and tug the man's trousers down to his ankles. Then Clayton would suddenly appear in the role of her outraged husband, threatening divorce with the hapless victim as co-respondent. The man, mindful of his wife and reputation, would usually promptly settle with whatever cash he was carrying. If he didn't, Clayton would beat him up and rob him.

Such beatings were also occasionally extended to Jean herself when she displeased Clayton. The sore on her nose was a relic of such a thrashing. It had been inflicted by a ring on Clayton's finger as he gave her a black eye. On the occasion of a recent badger game she had upset him by selecting a victim who had turned out to be too tough to handle.

Throughout their partnership Clayton had spent her immoral earnings on gambling, at which he had a conspicuous lack of success. And now, to cap it all, he had betrayed her.

Norman Andrews was a different type altogether. Although only five-foot-five, he was tough as they come, a hardened criminal frightened of no one. Wounded in action at Tobruk, he had subsequently been discharged from the forces when the Australian Army found him to be more trouble than he was worth — he was constantly going absent without leave.

Clayton had first met him in jail, and their chance encounter at Melbourne races had renewed their friendship. Both had lost heavily backing losers and they decided to team up, Andrews lending his muscle to Clayton's and Jean's badger games. The three had carried out two of these before Pop Kent became their victim. A young doctor and a chef had reported being robbed by them, and the police had been on the look-out for the trio.

The full extent of the torture suffered by Pop Kent became apparent at his inquest when Dr. Bowden detailed the victim's injuries. He said that two bloodstained penknives found in the room could have been responsible for some of Pop's face wounds. His abdominal wall and left thigh had been severely bruised in addition to his other injuries, and he had finally been manually strangled.

As each wound was described the three suspects nudged each other and laughed.

Committed for trial, they stepped into the dock at

Melbourne's Criminal Court on March 20th, 1950. Clayton and Jean then sat holding hands.

Repudiating his signed statement, Clayton told the court, "I turned like a yellow dog." Just about everything he'd told Mooney, he said, was untrue. He said that in fact he and his two companions had left Kent's home at 7 p.m.

Jean Lee claimed that Kent was "very well" when she left his room. She said she had been hysterical when she "made that confession."

Andrews continued to deny any involvement with either the robbery or the murder.

In his summing-up Mr. Justice Gavan Duffy told the jury: "When you find three people together who have been in the room where a bloody attack takes place later on, and then find them with what are said to be marks of violence on their hands and blood on their clothes, then the thing is too much of a coincidence to be treated as anything except strong proof that they were there and took part in the attack."

On March 25th it took the jury less than three hours to decide that all three defendants were guilty of William Kent's murder.

"I didn't do it! I didn't do it!" sobbed Jean Lee, collapsing into her lover's arms.

"You team of idiots!" Clayton shouted at the jury. "May your next feed choke you, you swine!"

Andrews, asked if he had anything to say, said, "Not at this juncture, no."

The judge then told the trio that they had been found guilty "on the strongest evidence, and I thoroughly agree with the verdict."

As the three were in turn each sentenced to death, Clayton spat at the jury, shouting: "Why don't you hang that lying swine Currer and those bastards?"

Appeals were made by the trio's defence lawyers to the Court of Criminal Appeal on the grounds that the confessions had been obtained under duress when the suspects were drunk and semi-hysterical.

In the courtroom on June 23rd the three defendants stood tensely awaiting the outcome. In a two-to-one majority decision the appeal judges ruled that the police had obtained the suspects' statements improperly; the statements from one prisoner being used to extract confessions from the others. The convictions were set aside and a new trial was ordered.

Jean Lee was exultant. "I knew it!" she cried, throwing her arms round Clayton and kissing him passionately. But her jubilation was premature. The Appeal Court's ruling was overturned by the High Court and the death sentences were restored.

Now 31 but looking 40, Jean Lee had become a shadow of her former self. As the date set for the trio's execution drew nearer she alternated between hysterical raving, violent attacks on her female warders, and abject begging for alcohol.

Clayton and Andrews were reported to have fallen out in jail, and on January 4th, 1951, their prison governor disclosed that Andrews had written a letter to the Inspector-General of Prisons, giving an account of the murder.

His letter said he had been pouring drinks when he heard Jean say, "Quick, Bobby!" He looked round and saw Pop Kent holding her arm. Clayton then punched the old man in the face.

Andrews claimed he asked what was going on and Clayton explained that Kent had caught Jean trying to rob him. They decided to tie their victim to his chair to give them time to get away safely.

Andrews wrote that he was tearing up a sheet to effect this when there was a knock at the door. He opened it and stepped outside to find the caller was one of Kent's woman friends from across the street, wanting a drink. He told her she couldn't come in as Kent was having a private party, and he then escorted her out to the street. When he returned to the room Kent was lying on the floor and Jean was kneeling beside him, crying.

"I said, 'What's wrong now?' and Clayton said, 'While you were talking to that woman out there, he [Kent] tried to make a noise to attract her attention and I had to stop him. I caught him around the throat and I think I held him too hard.'"

Andrews's letter went on to say that he found that Kent was dead. When he told Clayton he had killed him, Clayton replied, "I was afraid of that. I only meant to stop him singing out. I didn't mean to choke him."

The letter received only brief publicity. It seemed to be an attempt by Andrews to exculpate himself, and it failed to account for the extent of Pop Kent's injuries, which indicated prolonged torture.

Despite protests from opponents of capital punishment, it seemed clear that the executions would go ahead. Jean Lee would be the first woman to be hanged in Victoria for 56 years. In her cell she told a woman warder: "I just didn't do it. I haven't enough strength in my hands to choke anyone. Bobby was stupid, but the old man was trying to yell for help. None of us meant to kill him."

She was put under sedation.

Three days before the date set for the hangings a man with a weatherbeaten complexion arrived at Pentridge Prison where the three suspects awaited execution. To remain anonymous he wore welder's-style goggles and a tweed cap pulled well down. He was Australia's chief executioner, also employed as principal warder at another jail.

Jean Lee was the first to go to the gallows on Monday, February 19th, 1951. She was under such heavy sedation that some wondered if she knew what was happening as she shuffled under escort to a double cell near the scaffold. Regulations required Sheriff William Daly to read aloud to her the charge on which she had been convicted and sentenced. But on seeing the hangman and his assistant — both goggled and wearing felt hats — she collapsed. A doctor examined her and found she was in a coma.

The execution nevertheless went ahead. The sheriff read

out the details of her conviction and sentence. She could not have heard a word of this — if she had, she would have spotted a mistake. The document read by the sheriff had got the date of her sentencing wrong — it was wide of the mark by 19 days.

Instead of pinioning her arms behind her back, because she was comatose the executioner knelt and pinioned them in front of her. He and his assistant then fastened her feet together with a strap, put the white hood on her head and carried her from the cell to the gallows, where she was placed on a chair on the trap-door. Her head drooped to her chest and the hangman had to pull it back in order to tighten the noose behind her left ear.

The flap of the hood which was to cover her face had been left open. At a signal from the sheriff the executioner dropped the flap to obscure her face, jumped back from the trap-door, pulled the lever, and Jean Lee and the chair plummeted out of sight. The chair had been secured to the scaffold by a cord, and although it plunged with her the two parted company before the end of the drop.

Two hours later Robert Clayton and Norman Andrews, both mildly sedated, walked unaided to the scaffold. During their time together in the condemned cell Clayton had nicknamed Andrews "Charlie." Now as they stood side by side on the trap-door, he said, "Goodbye, Charlie."

"Goodbye, Bobby," Andrews replied.

Then the lever was pulled and both plunged to their deaths. But for their association with Jean Lee, the execution of such small-time crooks would no longer be remembered. Their date with the scaffold is still recalled, however, because their red-headed partner had made history. Jean Lee had become the last woman to be hanged in Australia.

13

THE FOXES IN THE WOOD MURDER

Brian Marriner

***A killer without qualms; cold,
calculating and merciless***

On the evening of September 5th, 1992, a middle-aged
couple, Mr. and Mrs. Robert Wignall, stood arm-in-
arm in Sayes Wood near their home in Addlestone,
Surrey, on the fringes of London. Bob Wignall was a
chronic asthmatic who was unable to fulfil his wife's sexual
needs, but he made up for this with numerous acts of
kindness and shows of affection. He had discovered the joy
of feeding fox cubs in the woods, and had fixed up a
spotlight to attract them. He thought his wife enjoyed
these little nocturnal outings.

In fact, Sandra Wignall found his affection and kindness
boring. What she yearned for was raw sex in its starkest
form. But now, on another walk in the woods to feed the
foxes, she pretended to share his simple pleasure. They
had been married for just nine months and some show of
affection was expected.

Tenderly, Sandra Wignall knelt before her husband and
performed oral sex on him. Breathing heavily from both
chronic asthma and sheer bliss, Robert Wignall was too
distracted to notice a flash of a spotlight then the two men

who crept up on him out of the dense undergrowth.

They attacked him mercilessly, beating him over the head. He didn't go down immediately. They never do. He tried to fight back and there was a brief scuffle during which he received three stab wounds, two of them to the heart. One of the attackers was unaware that he had lost his gold bracelet in the struggle, before Bob Wignall fell dead at their feet. That bracelet was to become a vital clue in the case.

The woman hesitated for a time, and then ran back to her home and telephoned the police, sobbing hysterically as she related what had happened. Police officers were soon on the scene, comforting her and trying to get good descriptions of the assailants. But she said it had been too dark to see anything distinctive, although she claimed there had been *three* attackers.

Her story was that while she and her husband were innocently feeding fox cubs in the woods, three youths approached them, asking them if they had seen a lost boxer dog. Then, for some inexplicable reason, the youths suddenly turned and attacked Bob, one of them with a knife. He shouted to her to run and hide, which she did. While hiding she heard Bob cry: "Get off my chest." She said that when she returned to her husband's side she bumped into three youths and asked them if it was they who had attacked her husband. They assured her they had not, and escorted her to a neighbour's house, from which the police were called.

Later that month, Sandra Wignall was seen by viewers of ITV's *Crime Monthly*, being interviewed about what had become known as the "Foxes in the Woods" murder. Tearfully, she appealed for witnesses of her husband's savage slaying to come forward, as she begged for the brutal killers to be caught.

But she was lying. Like so many killers she had used television to try to present herself as the innocent party, but this was a charade. She had planned her husband's death, orchestrated the attack — flashing the spotlight had been the signal for the killers to strike — and the oral sex had been a deliberate distraction. She had wanted her husband dead for the insurance money on his life, and because she had a secret lover who was badly in debt. She was that rare creature, a killer without qualms; cold, calculating and merciless.

Contrary to what popular detective fiction would have you believe, very few murderers actually *plan* their deed. To plot the death of another human being takes a special kind of person; one without conscience, without heart. Sandra Wignall was just such a woman. By coincidence, the man she took as a lover after the death of her first husband in 1985 had himself been convicted of murder in 1971 and had served 11 years of a life sentence. Here was a man with whom she could not only share the heights of erotic ecstasy, but also one with whom her pillow-talk could quite easily turn to murder plots. The devil himself could not have arranged a more evil partnership.

Her lover, six years younger than herself, was a chauffeur living in Ruislip, West London. He was short, podgy, bald, and wore spectacles. But he was street-wise, and his criminal background made him even more attractive to Sandra Wignall, who came from a somewhat higher social stratum. Terence Bewley, 42, had a Svengali-like hold over Sandra, to such an extent that he was able to make her take part in group-sex, make love in the back of Rolls-Royce cars, and even turn up to meet him — on his instructions — wearing nothing but a fur coat.

It wasn't that Sandra Wignall was sexually inexperienced. She had enjoyed several lovers before Bewley, but she became obsessed with him, because he knew exactly what she wanted and which buttons to press.

Perhaps Sandra Wignall came up with the idea of murder to force Bewley's hand, to link him inextricably to her. They would be joined by blood — the blood of an honest and good man who had never realised the kind of woman he had married.

Sandra had met Robert Wignall, a painter and

decorator, in 1990. Aged 55, he was mourning the death from cancer of his wife, Rose, a year earlier.

He was fond of walking his dog in woodland near his home in Addlestone, and it was during one of these strolls that he met Sandra Quartermaine, as she was then, also exercising her dog. She seemed an attractive woman in her late forties, but had he looked closer he would have seen a hard-bitten blonde. It was a chance meeting. They chatted. Then they looked forward to the daily meetings, and romance blossomed.

Sandra was working part-time as a cleaner, although she later got a job as a barmaid in a Virginia Water pub to help make ends meet. To a fellow-barmaid she confided her most intimate secrets, telling her of her passion for Terry Bewley and showing her semi-nude photographs that he had taken of her in the back of a Rolls Royce. Then she talked about Bob Wignall, saying he wanted to marry her. When the friend asked: "What about Terry?" Sandra replied: "I still love him, but Bob is too good to lose."

After the abrupt end of her relationship with Bewley, and perhaps on the rebound, Sandra went to see Bob at his home and had sex with him. Bob managed the act, despite his asthma, but wasn't particularly athletic in bed. At that time it didn't matter to Sandra. The sex had been a cold and calculated act, designed to entice him into her web. He was too good to lose because he had money and represented security. In August, 1991, a little over a year after they had first met, Robert Wignall left his own house and moved in with Sandra at her home in Rowhurst Avenue, Addlestone.

He had been devoted to his first wife and missed her terribly. His three children and five grandchildren could not compensate for her loss. To find a new love in his life seemed like a slice of good fortune. He married Sandra on Christmas Eve, 1991.

Just nine days after the wedding, Terry Bewley came back into Sandra's life, and their torrid affair began all over again. A friend in whom she confided advised her to stop seeing Bewley, but Sandra said simply: "I can't." And she couldn't. She was enslaved by physical lust.

For a time, the murder plot fooled experienced detectives. But there had been clues at the scene which had puzzled them, little inconsistencies which made them suspicious. Why had the victim been found with his fly unzipped? Why hadn't the mysterious killers attacked Mrs. Wignall too? What could have been their motive? They hadn't even robbed the victim.

Investigators worked on the theory that the killers were men from Sandra's past who had been motivated by jealousy. They started digging into the background of her former lovers, and when they came up with the name of Terence Bewley, they knew they were on the right scent.

There was the fact that Bewley was a convicted murderer. Then the fact that he was divorced and was deeply in debt, having been out of work for seven months and owing mortgage arrears of £15,000. His total debts amounted to almost £90,000, and Sandra Wignall had loaned him £4,000 to help him out, and at one stage had even considered selling her house to bail him out of his financial mess.

Within two days of the murder, Sandra Wignall contacted her husband's insurers, demanding immediate payment of the £21,000 due on his death. It was odd behaviour for a grieving widow...

Then there was the fact that the three youths Sandra Wignall claimed to have bumped into in the woods actually existed. They were traced and gave convincing statements about their innocence. But they also added something very interesting. While in the woods they had seen two men acting suspiciously who, once they realised they had been seen, disappeared hurriedly. So it was *two* attackers, not three. Why had Sandra lied?

Another clue was found in Mr. Wignall's clothing. Caught up in it was a gold bracelet bearing the initial "H". When the case was featured on the television programme *Crime Monthly*, with a full reconstruction of the crime, viewers were asked to phone in with any information they might have.

One caller with an obviously bogus foreign accent rang to say the police should look for two attackers, not three. He also hinted that Mrs. Wignall was herself involved in the murder plot. Eventually, after arranging a meeting in a pub with the officer in charge of the murder inquiry, Detective Superintendent Pat Crossan, and failing to turn up, the caller rang again. This time he gave his name. He was the boy friend of one of Bewley's relatives.

The story he told did not surprise Pat Crossan, who had always had his suspicions. On the face of it, it appeared to be a senseless crime, reflecting a sick society in which mindless cruelty and violence had become commonplace.

Such crimes are indeed committed, but in the detective's experience every killer had a motive, however well disguised. It was with great interest, therefore, that he listened to what the young man had to say. He told the detective he lived in Ruislip with Bewley. On the night of September 4th, which was a relative's 21st birthday, a party was held in the house. Among the guests was a strange man, a friend Bewley had made in prison. He was tattooed and talked tough, although he had no record of violence. He was just a petty thief. That night he muttered loudly about "sorting out" Mr. Wignall. And that same night a sharp kitchen knife disappeared from the house.

The boy friend knew that Sandra Wignall had been to the Ruislip house for sex sessions with Bewley, who had boasted of this. The detective listened attentively. Could he remember the name of the mystery guest? It was Harry something, he said.

And "H" was the initial on that gold bracelet ...

Bewley was put under close surveillance, and this led the police to Harry Moult, 42, from Ladywood, Birmingham. Meanwhile, Sandra Wignall was questioned about her husband's murder once again. It was hard to pin her down because she kept changing her story ...

She claimed, for example, that she had lost contact with

Bewley and had not seen him since March 1991. But the police were able to trace numerous telephone calls between the pair, and had evidence of many meetings in the month before Mr. Wignall's death.

If anyone was going to crack the case, it was always going to be Detective Superintendent Pat Crossan, a graduate of the FBI Academy who had spent over 20 years with the Surrey police after leaving his native Ireland. One of his favourite sayings was that in every murder "there are many victims. There are the relatives of the dead man, and the relatives of the murderers, too." This was the kind of perceptive remark which is foreign to many police officers. All her life Sandra Wignall had used men for sex. Now she had come up against Crossan, a man who was to destroy her.

She was arrested and taken to a police station for questioning. Also arrested in the same swoop were Bewley and Moult. Pat Crossan applied to a magistrate at Chertsey for an extension to the time allowed to question the trio, and this was granted. Put under enough pressure, one of them was bound to crack.

For a time all three remained silent, refusing to answer any questions. Then Moult asked to see Crossan and told him: "I want to get something off my chest. You know my record: I'm a thief, not a violent man ..." He then told about the murder of Bob Wignall.

Bewley had recruited him, as an old prison mate, to take part in the attack which Moult was told was meant simply to frighten Wignall. Everything was arranged. Sandra Wignall would see that the victim was in the woods at the right time, and would flash the fox-light to let them know when to strike. But when they attacked the victim he fought back, biting Bewley. Moult admitted he might have stabbed Bob Wignall "in a panic."

Afterwards, Moult returned to Birmingham, where he burned his clothing to destroy any forensic traces and dumped the murder knife in a nearby canal. Moult insisted that he believed they only intended to terrify

Wignall, and "it was never the plan that he should be killed." Having unburdened himself, Moult burst into tears, and Detective Superintendent Pat Crossan found himself having to comfort a self-confessed killer...

A call to the West Midlands Police sent them trawling the canal in question, from which they recovered two safes, dozens of supermarket trolleys — and the murder knife.

Faced with the evidence against them, the trio eventually talked.

The police discovered that Sandra stood to gain more than the £21,000 insurance on her husband's life. As his house was under a compulsory purchase order, she stood to inherit up to £100,000 for her performance in the woods.

Bewley himself was contemptuous under interrogation, saying that he had never loved Sandra, whom he described as his "old bird," and he had no intention of forming a permanent relationship with her. He described their affair as "on and off, and very, very casual."

It was Harold Moult who talked most. He described the killing in detail, saying that Bewley drove him to the woods, where together they confronted Bob Wignall. He went on: "Terry said something to him, and the next thing I knew they were on the floor fighting. I stepped in. I hit him. Terry hit him. I think I hit him with a piece of wood over the head.

"They were scuffling on the floor. I saw a knife and I am not sure if I picked the knife up and the bloke came at me. I might have stabbed him. I am not sure. I heard him say, 'Don't stab me.' It seemed like a long time but it was seconds."

The full sordid story of sex in the suburbs, with evidence suggesting that Addlestone was some kind of Peyton Place — where passions run high and women confide intimate details of their sex lives to their hairdressers — was outlined at Court Six at the Old Bailey when the trial of the trio began on October 26th, 1993.

Sandra Wignall, Terence Bewley and Harold Moult all pleaded not guilty to the charge of murder. Mr. Timothy Langdale QC, prosecuting, said it was a case of "lust and greed." Robert Wignall had been "an honest, everyday, decent sort of bloke — a kind, good-humoured man." He had died, the prosecution said, never knowing that his wife was having an affair or planning to cash in on his life insurance, taken out just six months before his death.

Mr. Langdale said that Sandra Wignall gave the impression of being happily married, "and there is no doubt that her husband loved her and was happy. But her marriage was not the blissful, perfect one which she chose to present at times to some people. She told one friend she found it difficult being with her husband all the time, and that their sex life was not so active because of his asthma."

Her story that her husband had been killed by three youths was "a complete fiction," Mr. Langdale continued. "Sandra Wignall had lured her husband to that place in the wood, knowing he was going to be done to death, and in the hope of lulling him into a false sense of security, she had gone so far as to be performing oral sex on him as the attack happened."

Describing Bob Wignall's death as "a tragedy," Mr. Langdale added: "The tragedy is that he never realised the truth about his wife. He never knew that Sandra Wignall was bored with her life with him and he never knew that she was possessed by what might be fairly called an obsession with Bewley." But, he said, "There is some evidence that towards the end of his life he was beginning to have some suspicions. Two days before he died Mr. Wignall found her car mileage, which he had begun to check, did not tally with the distances on "shopping trips" when she was really going to Ruislip to have sex with Bewley."

Sandra Wignall "was a woman to whom it seems sex was all-important." She had had five lovers before meeting Bewley, but "although she might fall for a number of men, there was one man who was a special object of desire to her, one man who seemed to have a hold over her that had led her always to do his bidding. That man was Terence Bewley. Bewley controlled her sex life to such an extent that, at his behest, she had sex with other men in front of him."

Describing how, after just nine days after her marriage to Bob Wignall, Bewley had reappeared in her life and their affair resumed, Mr. Langdale went on: "She said that marrying Bob had been a mistake. She had leapt into things too quickly and she was sad and miserable."

Bewley, who had previously refused to let her know where he lived, and had never taken her out, now allowed her to visit him at his home in Ruislip. She would sometimes drive there for sex after dropping her husband off at work. They continued meeting in secret, at least twice a week.

"She was besotted with him," Mr. Langdale said. "Happy when she saw him, and depressed when she did not."

Describing the investigation which had led to the arrest of the three people in the dock, Mr. Langdale said: "Sandra Wignall repeatedly changed her story in interviews with the police, but eventually confessed to arranging her husband's murder in a conversation with two of her relatives after she had been charged with murder."

Sitting in the dock in a red suit, her blonde hair swept tightly back Sandra Wignall appeared to be unmoved as she took occasional notes and shared jokes with the prison officer sitting next to her. Bewley sat a few feet away, but the couple did not look at each other, although Bewley and Moult spoke to each other occasionally.

The three youths who were in Sayes Wood at the time of the murder went into the witness box to tell of having seen two men "walking away quickly" from the scene of the crime. They had been illuminated by the spotlight which Mr. Wignall had erected to view the foxes.

One of Sandra Wignall's neighbours told the court

about conversations she had had with Sandra Wignall. She said Sandra described meeting Bewley at garages where the Rolls-Royces he drove in his work were kept. "She met him to have sex in the Rolls-Royces in the garages, and she showed me a couple of photographs of her in the cars dressed in her underwear."

The witness said that Sandra had told her about one occasion when she was invited out by Bewley and a friend. "She thought she was going out for a drink, but she was taken to this man Bill's house in Fulham. They all had drinks and one of them, Bill, took her blouse off and instigated having sex with her with Terry Bewley present. A short time later, when Bewley was abroad, Bill invited her over again and they had sex."

When Bewley found out, said the witness, "he was very angry. He came round and said he had a present for her. She told me he blindfolded her and tied her to the bed and brought in a man to have sex with her while Terry was present. It was someone she did not know. It happened again, once. She thought it was a different man — one had a moustache and the other did not."

She said that Sandra had once confided to her that Bewley had asked her to go to meet him at the garage wearing just a coat, with nothing on beneath. But her car broke down on the way and her state of undress "left her extremely distressed the morning after."

On the 19th day of the trial, the jury returned with unanimous verdicts of guilty of murder against all three defendants. Judge Neil Denison handed down three life sentences without comment. Usually in such cases a judge will make some remarks condemning the acts of the murderers. In this instance he may have felt that such words would be wasted on defendants beyond redemption.

Relatives of the murdered Bob Wignall hugged each other as the trio were led from the dock.

Outside the court Detective Superintendent Pat Cross-an described Sandra Wignall as a "cold, calculated and cunning woman." Then he added: "It has been a very traumatic time for the family. I hope they will now be able to start rebuilding their lives."

Typically, he was thinking of the other victims in the case. He also revealed that neither Wignall or Bewley had shown any sign of remorse.

What motivated Sandra Wignall's sexual behaviour? Psychologists tell us that nymphomaniacs are deeply unhappy women driven by a basic insecurity which makes them crave sex like a drug. It is an endless quest for something which doesn't exist for them: real love.

Sandra Wignall had two marriages behind her when she met Bob Wignall, but one man was never — could never — be enough. A friend confirmed that Sandra Wignall used to pick up young men when Bob was out and take them home for sex. She once spent an entire week cruising around picking up young men at random for sex in the back of her car. On another occasion she told the same friend: "I am going to make love to any man driving a red car tonight ..."

Her addiction to sex was insatiable, even becoming part of her murder plot with the performance of oral sex in the last moments of her husband's life.

She later told a friend, "He died happy." And, by her standards, he did.

14
PSYCHO WOMAN

Bill Kelly

**"A woman who is married to a strong,
sexy, handsome man like my husband will
do just about anything to prevent him from
running off with another female"**

WHAT HAPPENS when one fitness freak pairs-up
with another? It can be a recipe for disaster, as
tough-as-they-come Ray McNeil and his muscle-bound
bride were to discover ...

Thirty-four-year-old Sally McNeil was a nationally
known amateur body-builder about to turn pro. Her
husband Ray, five years her junior, was a former "Mr.
California" with hopes of breaking into show business.
The couple had a comfortable apartment on South
Tremont Street in Vista, California, not far from Camp
Pendleton where they had met as marines.

Ray had already appeared in TV commercials, and the
success of his stand-up routine at La Jolla's Comedy Club
on Monday amateur nights convinced critics he was ready
for the big time. He usually opened and closed his act with
a limerick — such as, "There was a young lady named
Wall/Wore a newspaper dress to a ball/ The dress caught
on fire/And burned her entire/Front page, sporting section
and all."

"Ray is a very funny man," said the club's proprietor. "He tells jokes about his body-building ... he has a lot of promise."

Although the strong man and his bride were both striving separately for success, their devotion to each other was obvious in the early days of their marriage. They were often seen hugging or holding hands, and friends said that "Wherever Raymond is, Sally won't be far behind."

As far as those friends could tell, the couple's inter-racial marriage of a white woman and a black man seemed to be going well.

Sally had always been attracted to big, athletic men, but her first marriage to a professional footballer had more ups and downs than a theatre-goer in an aisle seat. According to her divorce papers, the husband had used Sally as a punch-bag. An affidavit alleged that during one fracas he broke her big toe and put a gun to her head, threatening to pull the trigger. But the police learned that Sally's domestic battles with her first husband were not all one-sided.

Shortly after their divorce, a meeting of the couple to discuss their children once again ended in violence. Sally's former husband told the police that she punched him in the face, smashed the windscreen of his car with a metal bar and threatened to shoot him with a loaded pistol.

Sally denied the charges. But at one point in her interrogation she remarked, "A woman who is married to a strong, sexy, handsome man like my husband will do just about anything to prevent him from running off with another female."

She was arrested on a vandalism charge. The gun was never found.

The incident occurred in August 1990 at the South Tremont Street flat that Sally now shared with her new husband Raymond. During the day it was a quiet residential neighbourhood peopled by retired senior citizens, married working couples and families whose children walked to schools unafraid. But that part of Vista had its dangers at night. South Tremont was a dimly-lit side street with dark alleys and dismal, dormant apartment houses with shadowy carports. At night the safest place was behind locked doors.

But the demon that was out to get Raymond McNeil did not lurk in the shadows of the carports, or beneath the glare of the bright lights of the city streets. Raymond's high-risk area was his own home.

There is a saying that jealousy is a dragon which slays love under the pretence of keeping it alive. Several of Raymond's buddies said that was what broke up his increasingly stormy marriage to Sally. Raymond, they said, appeared worn-out and devastated by the bickering that went on behind closed doors. Having constantly accused her first husband of cheating on her, Sally now gave Raymond the same treatment.

She seldom let him out of her sight. If he went out for a newspaper she wanted to know what kept him so long. She wanted to know if he'd seen any sexy women in the shop. If he was late coming home from the Comedy Club, he went through the third degree.

"She is a real 'Psycho woman,' " said one neighbour of Sally McNeil.

Ray used the family bickering as material for his Comedy Club routine.

"We used to keep a diary of our quarrels," he mused, "but we had to give it up — it turned into a scrapbook ... my marriage is proof that two can live as bitter as one."

Another time he quipped, "My wife and I are inseparable. It took two policemen to pull us apart."

But Sally's children didn't think it was funny, and one relative observed, "Sally is an intelligent woman. She's not the raving lunatic others make her out to be. But something is definitely wrong mentally."

A bartender who had served the McNeils many times said that Raymond tried to work, support, provide a home, and sex, but nothing he did seemed to please Sally.

Ray tried to persuade his wife to seek psychiatric help,

but she refused.

"I'm just whipped," he told a friend. "I can't continue like this. Sally needs help."

One night the police received an anonymous tip that she had threatened to kill herself. Another evening while Ray was doing his stand-up comedy routine he received an urgent call. Sally had phoned the emergency services saying she was ill and needed help. She asked the police to call Ray and bring him to the hospital. The doctors could find nothing wrong with her. She later confessed that she'd had visions of Ray with another woman at the club and wanted him home.

Finally the constant bickering got the better of Raymond and he decided to leave. When Sally came home from the shopping he was already packed and on his way out. She attacked him in a frenzy, scratching, biting and kicking him. She called him names that would make a truck driver blush. Ray fought her off, stormed out and started up his truck.

Sally ran out, jumped on the bonnet and banged on its windscreen until her hands bled. Then she ran back to their first-floor apartment and threw an entire weight set over the balcony.

During the early morning hours, when Ray left the Comedy Club after doing his routine, he never knew what to expect. One night he found every tyre on his truck had been sliced to ribbons. Another night every wire under the bonnet had been pulled out or cut. On a third occasion his windscreen was smashed. A brick was found on the front seat. Then the vehicle went up in flames and Ray's insurance company dropped him like a hot potato.

When he went over to Sally's apartment for a showdown she had him arrested. A restraining order against him stated that he had knocked her around.

But further questioning of Sally's friends by a newspaper reporter produced a different picture of the female body-builder.

At around midnight on July 15th, 1990, police were

summoned to Sally's apartment by her daughter. The seven-year-old said that she and her five-year-old brother had been left alone at home by their mum.

Police found the apartment "dirty, unkempt, with dirty clothing piled high and rubbish thrown all over every room." Officer D. Cox wrote in his log: "There was no fresh food in the kitchen. I noticed that cookies and ice cream were out on the table, and appeared to be the only food available."

When Sally got home after midnight the police were waiting with a social worker. As they attempted to speak to her she became violent. She resisted their attempts to question her children. Eventually they calmed her by threatening to arrest her and put her children into protective custody. She told the officers that the children had been left alone because she was stranded in a car park with a flat tyre and no spare.

When the social worker indicated that she would have to take the children into custody until the situation was straightened out in court, Sally went berserk. In his report. Officer Cox wrote: "McNeil is a body-builder and is very strong." He said she tried to throw his partner over her shoulder and fought with the ferocity of a bulldog. "The officers finally subdued her by spraying Mace in her face."

She was placed under arrest and rushed downtown. The following day she was released after paying a stiff fine. A reluctant judge gave her children back to her with a warning.

In another situation in 1990 the district chairman of the National Physique Committee barred Sally from body-building competitions for a year after she beat up a female spectator during a body-building event. Sally had suspected the woman was having an affair with her husband.

Two more knock-down cat-fights with females over the affections of Sally's husband added to the list of violent episodes, and the suspicion that she was a walking time-bomb was strengthened again in 1993 when she was convicted of yet another assault on a female who had looked at her husband twice.

Meanwhile Ray McNeil seemed to be on his way to stardom. He appeared in a commercial seen by millions nationwide. It featured Hollywood stars Lloyd Bridges and Jason Alexander, and Bridges spent time discussing Ray's future in show business.

But it would never happen. It all came to an end the weekend he was scheduled to compete in the South Florida Professional Invitation body-building tournament. *Muscle and Fitness* magazine reported that this would be Ray's first major competition for more than a year.

Relatives from as far away as Pennsylvania were planning to attend. All the McNeils would be there. But not Raymond. On St. Valentine's Day, 1995, his life ended with a frantic phone call to Oceanside police from a next-door neighbour who had been woken by the McNeils' two children screaming and pounding on her door. One was crying: "Oh, my God! Oh, my God! Let me in! My mom shot my dad, my dad!"

Two patrolmen who arrived shortly after 10.40 p.m. met Sally McNeil at the door and stepped inside to examine the victim. Although hit in the face and stomach by two shotgun blasts, Ray was still alive. Three minutes later paramedics whisked him to a nearby hospital where he died while undergoing surgery.

Under questioning, Sally decided to tell the truth — sort of. She stumbled through her sentences, was hesitant and evasive. Finally after an hour of listening to Sally answer, "I can't remember" and "I don't know," the detectives shook their heads wearily. They told her she was under arrest for the murder of her husband.

At the Vista police station Sally was nervous but under control. She said she shot her husband in self-defence after he hit, beat, and sexually assaulted her. She was booked for first-degree murder and held without bail.

At her trial before Superior Court Judge Laura Palmer Hammes, prosecutor Goldstein said there was no direct evidence to support Sally's claim that she had shot her husband in self-defence. He argued that even if the defence came up with evidence to substantiate her story, the real issue was that Mrs. McNeil should be punished for having taken a life. Whether she was or wasn't abused had "nothing to do with the fact that all she had to do was to call the police," Goldstein told the jurors.

Defence Attorney Bill Rafael countered by pointing out that a police officer who responded to the call reported that he had noticed choke-marks on Sally's neck.

Sally McNeil, clad in a dark blue dress, her blonde hair pulled back in a French braid, sat at the defence table listening to her mother testify how Sally phoned her immediately after the shooting: "Mom, I'm in big trouble. I shot Ray."

The witness told the court that her first reaction was: "What did you say?" And her daughter repeated, "I shot Ray. We had a fight and he was choking me and I shot him."

"She told me, 'I'm so sorry. I'm so terribly sorry. I'm going to be in jail for a long time."

The witness said she talked long-distance to the San Diego receiving home where Sally's children, 11 and nine, were being looked after. She told the court that her elder grandchild told her, "My dad came home late and my mom asked where he'd been . . . and he just ran at her and choked her and pushed her around." Later in her testimony Sally's mother said her granddaughter told her, "I heard a loud boom, and when I came out to see what the boom was, my dad was on the floor and I ran outside screaming."

Detectives testified that illegal anabolic steroids were a contributing factor to the young couple's violence towards one another.

Sergeant Rick Sing told the court that steroids were found in the apartment. He said Sally had admitted that she and her husband regularly took the muscle-enhancing drugs, which experts say cause aggression and violence.

The prosecuting attorney told jurors that the two quarrelled on the night of the killing, and Raymond went into the kitchen to make himself a sandwich. Sally had other plans. She went into the bedroom, loaded a double-barrelled shotgun and shot her husband. The blast lifted him off his feet and sent him flying over a kitchen table six feet away. He bled profusely from the abdomen and face and died two hours later.

A pathologist testified that the cause of death was bullet punctures to the lungs, head, abdomen, laceration of the brain and extensive blood trauma. Any of these could have killed the muscleman. The dead man's skin in both front and rear had been peeled off by the blast. His sex organs were torn and hanging loosely by flaps of skin to his body.

"He died a horrible death," the pathologist told the court.

After nearly three hours deliberation the jury found Sally McNeil guilty of second-degree murder.

Sentencing the muscle-woman to 19 years to life on April 19th, 1996, Judge Hammes said she was convinced that Sally was a battered woman, but that she was also violent herself.

"He did not deserve to die," Hammes said of the former body-building champion, "and he did not deserve to die in this way. His was a terrible death."

If you want your husband out of the way, don't do it yourself. . get the experts to do the job

15
DEATH OF A PRIVATE EYE

Brian Marriner

"Who killed Barry Trigwell? It could be one of fifty people"

PRIVATE detectives often work in sleazy settings, and some of the grime inevitably rubs off. That's how it was with Barry Trigwell, 44, known as "Barry the Bastard" both to fellow-investigators and his clients. He ran the Birmingham office of a national investigative agency and was known as a sharp, tough operator. His deputy was a former policeman, and in classic private eye tradition it was the deputy who made the grim discovery.

On the morning of February 7th, 1995, he drove to Trigwell's detached home in Fowey Close, Walmley, near Sutton Coldfield. He was due to pick up his boss for work, as he did every morning, but there was no response when he rang the doorbell. That was odd, as was the presence of Trigwell's kitten, mewing on the doorstep — it never went anywhere without its mother...

The deputy dialled his boss on his mobile phone, but got no reply. Now worried, he used his key to let himself into the house. Inside he found signs of disorder, with a trail of blood leading from the living-room of the rented house up to the bathroom. Gingerly following this trail, he found Trigwell lying in the bath, the now-cold water almost black from the blood which had run from his bludgeoned head. He was very dead.

Police detectives arrived and all the usual police things were done: the house was dusted for fingerprints and photographs were taken of the body. Trigwell was wearing his trousers but no shirt.

A colleague told the press: "He crossed a lot of people, and to them he was known as 'Barry the Bastard.' But he told his clients to call him God. Barry seemed to live for the adrenaline rushes. Wherever he went, intrigue followed. He was a short, stocky bloke who looked like the classic image of a Chicago gangster, but people respected him. He really enjoyed snatching children back from abroad after one of the parents had skipped the country. Barry has made many enemies in life."

There was no shortage of suspects — the problem was that there were too many people who had hated Barry's guts and had reason to seek revenge. Furthermore, Trigwell had previous convictions for blackmail and illegal possession of a firearm. So had he fallen foul of underworld contacts?

A routine part of the police investigation was to probe the victim's background and build up a profile. The portrait which emerged was not a pretty one. Short and thick-set, with a powerful build making him seem like a Bob Hoskins double, Trigwell had been married three times, his current wife having been in South Africa at the time of the murder. Trigwell was known to have been tight with money — he never tipped local taxi drivers. And he was tight-lipped, never saying much about his business.

The team investigating his murder worked out of Nechell's Green police station, a one-storey building in a drab, crime-ridden area. Detective Chief Superintendent Ken Evans had the task of trying to assemble the bits of the jigsaw puzzle that accompany any murder. This one was going to be more complicated than most. "It's a morass, a tangled web," Evans told reporters. "He's got a finger in that many pies ..."

At the time of his death Barry Trigwell held a second passport in another name and was investigating the laundering of drugs money and monitoring the import of arms into the Seychelles.

Detectives believed that whoever killed the private eye had probably been close to him, because there was no sign of forced entry. It was thought that the killer or killers may not have had murder in mind, but may have been intent on just giving Trigwell a warning by way of a punishment beating. The police believed that Trigwell had been coshed downstairs on the sofa, and when he recovered consciousness had staggered upstairs to the bath and had fallen in. He would have died from the head wounds alone, since his skull had been smashed in several places, but drowning could not be ruled out.

Inquiries continued, with the police sifting Trigwell's paperwork, tracing former clients who might bear a grudge, and trying to find out as much as they could about the dead man's current investigations.

They found that he had been a busy man. He had worked in Hong Kong, the Middle East, Texas, Africa, South Africa, the Seychelles — always on rough and dirty cases. It was known that he'd had some "dodgy dealings" with the Mozambique Government. And there was even gossip that he had made a small fortune by arranging "end jobs" — trade jargon for assassinations — and had incurred the wrath of Special Branch, who were never able to pin anything on him.

A colleague said: "He had been involved in cases all over the world, he has been caught in some heavy stuff, but this was supposed to be a quiet patch in his life."

The previous year Trigwell had been in Hong Kong, where he hired two heavies, booked flights back to the UK and then snatched a child from a flat, bringing him home to the estranged parent.

As one investigator put it: "Who killed Barry Trigwell? It could be one of fifty people."

Larger offices were sought for the investigators. The life

and death of Barry the Bastard were too complex to be handled from just a room or two.

In seeking a motive the first question detectives ask is: "Who gains?" The immediate suspect is usually the closest relative. In this case Barry's wife, Anne, in South Africa

They had learned that Trigwell's marriage had been unhappy. His wife had been having an affair with a man in South Africa — where she herself had been born — and although she swore it was over and she was no longer in contact with the man, the suspicious private eye had arranged to have his own phone bugged. His sister told the police that he had suspected someone was trying to kill him after he received mysterious phone calls from a South African man.

The wife stood to gain financially from her husband's death — a cool £380,000 from a life insurance policy — and there was evidence that she had previously threatened Trigwell's life . . .

A six-man team of detectives flew out to South Africa 10 days after the murder to gather evidence, but the vital clues lay closer to home.

It seemed that by bugging his own phone Barry Trigwell had fingered his killers, because the police were able to trace those calls from the mysterious South African man. Not that they needed to. Barry Trigwell had become suspicious of the South African's attempts to lure him to a rendezvous, and fearing the worst he had traced the number and passed it to his sister for use in the event of his death.

The calls had come from the local Clover Hotel, two miles from Trigwell's home, where two South African men had been staying. The bungling hit-men had even used their own names to register. The hotel staff implicated Anne Trigwell, describing her as a South African woman who had arrived at the hotel to drop off keys and £300 in a brown envelope for the two men. She had to deliver the cash along with her front-door key because the hit-men had blown their initial expenses on high living.

The seeds of the crime lay in South Africa, and the evidence necessary for a conviction came from there. It came in the person of a 26-year-old glamorous blonde, a former model and ex-porn queen who was the estranged wife of a South African underworld boss. In January 1995, at her home in South Africa, the woman who had once been a Penthouse "Pet of the Year" overheard her husband and Anne Trigwell plotting to have Barry Trigwell killed. Now she was willing to provide some of the missing pieces in the jigsaw and testify at any trial — but she herself was now in fear for her life.

Disenchanted by her husband and his criminal life-style, she had helped the South African police mount a sting operation to arrest him, but she failed to turn up at a trial in which he and two alleged hit-men were charged with conspiracy to commit murder. As a result, the trial collapsed. With the help of a business rival of her husband, the informer fled South Africa.

When contacted by British police she was touring Europe with an exotic dance troupe. After telling what she knew she returned to a hideout in Italy, guarded by a minder.

It had taken British detectives a long time to track her down, and they found her reluctant to talk. "It took hours of careful persuasion to get her to testify," said one. "She undoubtedly put herself at enormous risk. There is no doubt in my mind that threats were made against her by the criminal underworld." When she did begin to talk she had an amazing tale to tell.

Barry Trigwell had met his wife-to-be, Anne, while in South Africa working on a case. She had returned to live in South Africa after her second marriage broke down. She had bought a £400,000 house with a swimming pool outside Johannesburg and was mixing with the owner of a gambling casino. He was mixed up with many other rackets as well.

For a shrewd private eye Barry Trigwell was curiously

blind when it came to the personality faults in Anne. But then they were well suited, with a shared taste for gambling, sex and the high life. They were also both extremely arrogant.

After a tempestuous affair they travelled back to the UK together and were married at Birmingham Register Office in 1994, by which time Barry Trigwell was based permanently in England, building up a franchise of the national private detective agency and earning up to £3,000 a week. His bride rented out her mansion in South Africa and the newly-weds set up home in Sutton Coldfield. Barry Trigwell changed all his life insurance policies to make his new wife the beneficiary. But it took less than 12 months for the marriage to end in murder.

Barry Trigwell's sister told how at a dinner party two months before his death he had begun to suspect that his wife was having an affair with someone in South Africa, where she made regular visits on the pretext of visiting her daughter. He suggested that he might accompany her on her next South African trip.

The sister said: "She leaned across the table and grabbed him by the jumper and said, 'If you come to South Africa I will have you shot, and I know at least two people who will do it.'"

The problem for the British police lay in the fact that they could not arrest the two suspected hit-men, as they were back in South Africa and no extradition treaty exists between the two countries. But they could lay hands on the widow, who was in England for her husband's inquest — and to claim the insurance money.

It was her behaviour at that inquest which confirmed the suspicions of the murder team detectives. Detective Chief Superintendent Evans said later: "Inquests are very emotional times, but there was not a flicker of emotion on her face throughout." She was arrested immediately afterwards. During many police interviews she denied any knowledge of a contract out on her husband's life, and denied ever having threatened to kill him.

Ethel Anne Trigwell, 43, appeared in the dock at Birmingham Crown Court on July 8th, 1996, charged with the murder of her husband. She pleaded not guilty.

For the prosecution, Anthony Raggatt QC told the jury that the woman in the dock had been driven by motives of sex and money to hire two South African hit-men to murder her husband. He claimed she had paid £15,000 for the "hit." The other principals in the case had escaped justice as they could not be brought back from South Africa. Why had the murder taken place? Because the Trigwells' marriage had failed, she had a South African lover and she stood to benefit financially from her husband's death.

"Their marriage was disastrous and the romance did not last past the wedding ceremony," the prosecutor said. "As 1995 unfolded the marriage collapsed in ruins."

Mr. Raggatt continued: "Anne Trigwell wanted Barry dead for sex and money... her husband was worth a great deal more to her dead than alive."

The principal prosecution witness was the ex-porn queen from South Africa who had flow to Britain from the Continent to testify at the trial. She said that she and her former husband had rented Anne Trigwell's house in Johannesburg. Mrs. Trigwell later visited them, saying she had a problem with Barry and wanted to be separated.

The witness said that her own ex-husband bragged about his connections with hit-men and offered to help out. There had been four meetings between her husband and Anne Trigwell, and one involving the two hit-men. The original plan had been to shoot Barry Trigwell, but the two hit-men complained that he had too many neighbours, so they decided to do the job on the "inside." The deal was that the witness's ex-husband was to get Mrs. Trigwell's plush Johannesburg house for organising the killing, and the two men dispatched to Britain to carry out the crime were to split the money on offer — some 100,000 rand, or about £15,000.

Anne Trigwell could afford it — she stood to gain

£400,000 from insurance and mortgage bonds following her husband's death.

The witness said that after the killing she left her husband and made a statement to the South African police.

Cross-examining her, Mr. Michael Mansfield QC, defending, claimed that her ex-husband had approached another man to carry out the killing weeks before she had ever met Mrs. Trigwell. The defence counsel accused the witness of lying in order to cover up for someone in South Africa. The implication was that the witness's ex-husband had more cause to kill Barry Trigwell than had the victim's wife. Mr. Mansfield claimed that the witness and her ex-husband had "set up" Anne Trigwell to carry the can for a contract taken out on Barry Trigwell by someone else.

The witness retorted that her husband had threatened to have her killed if she testified against him. She said she had left him after he told her that Barry Trigwell was dead. "I was not happy about the murder story, we were not getting on and he was slapping me about." She said her husband told her that two hired hit-men had beaten Barry Trigwell to death after their gun failed to go off.

Word had reached her from her husband that she would not live if she testified, but she got protection from one of his business rivals who paid for a restraining order against him. She had fled South Africa after hearing about the murder, and after living in Italy for a time she had come to England just three days previously to testify at the trial. "I came especially to give evidence to get it over and done with, so I can get on with my life."

The court heard from hotel staff where the two South African hit-men had stayed. They testified to having seen Anne Trigwell at the hotel and said they became suspicious of the heavy brown envelope she dropped off for two men and opened it, thinking it might contain drugs. In it were house keys and £300.

The court heard that the white Fiat Punto car hired by the two men had been found, and forensic tests discovered traces of Barry Trigwell's hair and scalp on the back seat.

Anne Trigwell went into the witness box to tell how she met the man believed to have set up the assassination of her husband. She said she had told him that she was importing and exporting medical supplies and needed trucks for haulage. He said he might be able to help. Asked if he had boasted of Mafia connections or said he could have her husband killed, she replied, "No."

She told the jury that her marriage had broken down because her husband had been violent and abusive when drunk, and his sexual demands and habits offended her.

Summing-up, Mr. Justice Nelson said it was not in dispute that there had been a plot to kill Barry Trigwell, and he had been killed by at least two vicious blows to the head.

The evidence for the prosecution suggested that Anne Trigwell had delivered a key and money to the killers at a Walmley hotel and made threats to kill her husband in the presence of relatives. As for motive, "She wanted to rid herself of her hated husband and gain almost £400,000," the judge said. Anne Trigwell had admitted that she had spent the night prior to the murder with her lover.

The defence case was that Anne Trigwell had been framed by someone else who had planned the murder and needed to place the blame elsewhere.

Mr. Justice Nelson told the jury: "Only if you are sure she plotted the murder of her husband can you convict. Anything less and you should acquit."

At the end of the 14-day trial the jury deliberated for 14 hours. Then they delivered their unanimous verdict that the slim, black-haired wife was guilty of plotting the murder of her husband.

Sentencing the impassive woman in the dock to life imprisonment, Mr. Justice Nelson told her: "This was a cold, calculated offence, a chilling murder. You inspired and planned the death of your husband and you were actively involved in ensuring the killers were able to perform their gruesome and vicious task."

Throughout the trial Anne Trigwell had never shown the slightest flicker of emotion. For most of the time she looked bored.

However, there is one last twist to this extraordinary story. A prison officer met Anne Trigwell while she was being held at Risley Remand Centre and fell in love with her. An affair began between the couple, as a result of which the officer sacrificed his 17-year career for the woman he found "vulnerable and sensitive."

"I have always believed in her innocence and that she would not be convicted," he said. "I will wait for her. With luck she will be out in twelve years and we will both begin a new life in South Africa. From the moment I first kissed her I knew my career in the Prison Service was as good as over."

16

SEX, LIES AND MURDER

Charles Sasser

Florida's intriguing Barbara Bell case

SOBBING AS she identified herself as Barbara Bell, the woman telephoning the police in Tulsa, Oklahoma, was hysterical.

"Oh, my God! This is a nightmare!" she shrieked. "Help me! Help me! He's not awake. He's breathing. What do I do? Send me an ambulance."

The woman could then be heard wailing, "Don't die! Don't die!"

It was about 10.30 on that cold night of January 22nd, 1993, and emergency services sped to the house on East 66th Street on Tulsa's exclusive south side.

Patrol Corporal Paul Eskridge observed that the garage door hung open. New cars were parked in the drive. Lights inside the garage glared brightly upon the scene of the tragedy, exposing it for all the neighbours to see.

A petite woman with short, stylish auburn hair crouched by the garage. In her lap she cradled the handsome head of a well-dressed middle-aged man who appeared to be unconscious. Blood throbbed from an ugly bullet hole almost directly in the centre of his forehead. Both man and woman were spattered with bright blood.

"Things like this don't happen to people like me," the woman sobbed.

That plaintive phrase launched Tulsa detectives, led by veteran Homicide Sergeant Wayne Allen, on a case that seemed designed to prove that money cannot always buy happiness.

As 51-year-old Dr. Davis Lloyd Bell was rushed to hospital in a critical condition, the investigators began reconstructing the events which had led up to the bloody scene.

From the genteel front the Bells presented, an observer would conclude that they lived a charmed life. Dr. Bell was a highly successful orthopaedic surgeon. He and his wife, 46-year-old Barbara, headed an apparently ideal American family. They lived in an ideal house in the best part of the city, and were active in civic affairs.

Over the next few days, police questioned the Bells' friends and relatives, trying to determine what had happened to turn the lights off for a brilliant surgeon and his attractive wife.

One of Dr. Bell's associates described the surgeon as being "carefree and happy" in recent months. Bell, he said, was a private person who liked to study and to work with his computer.

"His mind was into medicine, and that's where he functioned day and night. He had a very high self-esteem about his abilities. Money was important to him, but his ego was more important still. Money was the way you kept score."

Other friends said that David Bell left the running of his home and the rearing of the children almost exclusively to his wife, while he immersed himself in his career.

The Bells had gone out for dinner with Carl and Freda Heinz early on the Friday evening of the shooting. During dinner, Carl Heinz had said that David had seemed rather "uncommunicative" with his wife over two forthcoming trips she proposed, but otherwise everything appeared normal.

The two couples returned to the Bell home after dinner. It was about 9 p.m. The Bells' teenage children were not at home. The men retired to Dr. Bell's computer room to talk. Shortly afterwards, Bell received a call.

Heinz recalled that the doctor said he had to go to the hospital for something minor.

The Heinzes then departed.

"My husband told me he had to go to the hospital," Barbara Bell subsequently explained. "I was very tired and was going to bed. I was going to call David at the hospital and ask him to wait up until our son came home. I called two hospitals and a pager company, and couldn't find him."

Investigators questioned switchboard operators at nearby St. Francis Hospital. The duty operator remembered a call for Dr. Bell. It had come in at 9.29 p.m. that Friday from "a lady asking him to call home."

Minutes later, the St. Francis emergency room secretary had received a similar call from a woman who identified herself as Mrs. Bell. She asked for Dr. Bell.

"I told her he wasn't here," the secretary recalled. "She said that he must be in surgery, so I transferred her up there. She called back and I put her on hold as I paged Dr. Bell. There was no response. When I looked down, the light wasn't flashing. She had hung up."

Then who, police wondered, had paged Dr. Bell at home at 9 p.m. and asked him to come to the hospital. Or was he paged to the hospital — and if not to there, then to where?

Dr. Marvin Rawls was one of the surgeons who worked on the critically wounded surgeon at the St. Francis emergency room, trying to save his life, but Bell died at 12.23 a.m. without regaining consciousness.

A few hours later Rawls and a group of the Bells' friends met the new widow to console her.

"I told her the children were fine and the house was secured," Rawls told reporters. "She asked, 'Where's Silkie?' At first I didn't know what she meant. She told me it was her dog."

He described Barbara Bell as "zombie-like. She seemed

catatonic. She stared into space."

On Sunday, when Dr. Rawls and friends met at the Bell residence to help the widow work out funeral arrangements, Barbara Bell seemed to have recovered. She said, "I have no remorse. I've done nothing wrong. It wasn't an accident. It was a mistake."

A man with a bullet hole between his eyes was a mistake?

To his surprise, Sergeant Allen discovered that both David and Barbara Bell had been hiding funds from each other. Bank records indicated that in October 1992 Barbara moved $100,000 from one account to another. David apparently had his own secret bank account containing $66,000.

His death left his widow with a windfall of $6 million — including $2.5 million in assets and $3.5 million in insurance.

Police also learned that each partner in the marriage had been plagued with emotional problems.

One of Dr. Bell's brothers would later testify that he and David had grown up in a "dysfunctional family" and had been estranged from each other for 21 years. When he learned of David's death he said he wasn't too surprised. His first reaction was, "That just fits our family. I think my father killed my mother."

As for Barbara Bell, records indicated that she took antidepressant drugs, headache medication and a sleeping aid.

Her attorney said that "the allegation that Mrs. Bell thrives on preferential treatment, has a litany of lawsuits, and runs off bill collectors with a burglar alarm is utterly unsubstantiated and flies directly in the face of the financial condition of the Bell family ... she categorically denies that she ever said she is the 'Leona Helmsley of Tulsa.' "

The so-called "Hotel Queen" Leona Helmsley was a self-described "rich bitch" who had been convicted and sentenced to prison for tax fraud in late 1992.

"The most spurious allegation," Barbara's attorney

continued, "is that Mrs. Bell has obtained, indirectly, over five million dollars as a result of David's death. The truth, of course, is that his death cost her about five million dollars ... and can be documented by agreements showing that the entire proceeds from insurance premiums have gone directly to her children, not her."

"They didn't have a marriage in the true sense," Barbara's friend Freda Heinz would subsequently testify. "They lived like brother and sister. They were like friends. They had no sexual relationship for twelve years ... Barbara asked David to go to Masters and Johnson (famed sex therapists). He always refused. That's what I would expect. He was very concerned that someone in the medical community would know what his private life was really like."

Heinz testified that Barbara had confided in her 10 years before that she was very unhappy in her marriage and had contemplated divorce. But then the unhappy woman had changed her mind.

"I'm not going to do this to my children," she had decided. "I don't want them to come from a broken home. He doesn't beat me, and he doesn't lie to me, and I'm going to make the best of it."

Five years later Heinz asked Barbara how much longer she intended to stay with her unresponsive husband.

"She said not until the kids were out of school would she even consider divorce ... Barbara was dramatic and very, very outspoken. She could rant and rave, and I always thought her bark was ferocious, but that's where it ended. They didn't have a lot of communication. It was not a close-knit relationship. They never touched each other or showed any affection at all."

Detectives discovered that David Bell had also considered divorce.

"My wife and I never do things together any more," he had complained to a friend, admitting that the only thing that kept him with Barbara was money. It would cost him $1 million to leave her, he calculated.

As far as police could determine, neither partner knew that the other had seriously contemplated divorce.

David, however, had also kept another, more devastating secret from his wife.

Barbara had no knowledge that her husband was having an affair at the time of his death, claimed her attorney.

But if Barbara Bell knew nothing about the affair, almost everyone else in the Bells' social circle did.

The Bells' accountant told the police that he found out about the doctor's extra-marital relationship in the autumn of 1992, about the time it began, but he did not tell Barbara. A friend of David from the gym where he worked out would later testify that David had told her on January 11th that he was having an affair with a nurse. A plastic surgeon recalled that David said he was "very much in love" with this woman.

Barbara Bell had apparently learned of the affair two days after her husband's death. A friend of hers told detectives: "She ran up to me. She was crying. She asked, 'David was having an affair?' She was in disbelief."

Sergeant Allen and his colleagues picked up the mystery girl friend's trail. They learned not only of deceit in the Bell household, but also of the fear.

"David had to hide the affair from Barbara," a family friend said. "He was afraid of her."

On the day before he was shot, Dr. Bell confided to another surgeon that his wife had threatened to kill him if he ever left her. Nevertheless, Bell said, he intended to divorce Barbara in order to be with his lover.

"He was very up," the surgeon-friend recalled. "He didn't think his wife knew anything specific about the affair. I told him to be careful."

Seven hours before his death, Dr. Bell had told another colleague that he was "in great fear of being killed" by his wife.

"You're joking!" the friend had responded with amazement.

"No, she means it," Bell had replied.

"If you have any guns in the house," the friend advised, "you'd better get rid of them."

The friend then recounted how Bell planned to leave his wife when she was out of town. He would get a security system and file a restraining or protective order to keep Barbara away from his office.

"These people had an unusual relationship," Barbara's lawyer conceded. "David Bell was having an affair with a young nurse whom he was quite enamoured of. He thought he loved her but was having difficulties making a decision. Over the months, he was in the process of having to choose between the other woman and his wife. He feared his wife would exact a heavy financial penalty."

Was the shooting an accident, a tragic mistake — or was it premeditated, cold-blooded murder?

Six million dollars was a lot of motive. So was an unfaithful husband.

Dr. Bell's lover turned out to be Pam Albright, a twice-divorced brunette with two young children. She later testified, "He said his wife had told him that if he ever left her she would kill him. He told me money was the only thing that kept him there ... Money was real important to him, as was I ... Money was who he was — how he wanted to express himself, how much money he had and how much he could make. I kept trying to make him understand why I needed to see beyond money."

She said Bell told her she was his first affair.

"I didn't believe him initially. He was well liked, attractive, and had been unhappily married for all those years. After I got to know him, it was really obvious he wasn't lying."

"Did you love Dr. Bell?" she was asked.

"I did."

"Did he love you?"

"He did."

Pam Albright revealed where David Bell went after being paged at home that Friday evening. She said that he had had himself paged as an excuse to leave home and visit her. He had called her for the last time from his car phone about 25 minutes before his death.

Detectives said there were apparently only two people at the Bells' home on that fateful night: David Bell and his wife. And now Barbara was expressing conflicting sentiments to friends which heightened police suspicion of her.

The shooting, she said, "was not an accident. An accident is when you walk into the bright sunshine and lightning strikes a tree and it falls on you. That's an accident. This was a mistake. He made a mistake. Any idiot knows you don't run towards a gun."

Crucial questions centred around a "half-cocked" 9MM Browning semi-automatic pistol that Detective Bart Dean found lying on a kitchen table on the night of the shooting. Dean said the weapon's magazine was fully loaded with 10 rounds, with a spent shell casing still in the chamber. Normally a semi-automatic ejects a spent round after it is fired.

The police department's weapons expert subjected the gun to various tests. The pistol had four safety mechanisms, he said, each of which must be released before the weapon could be fired. He soon concluded that the fatal bullet had been fired from that gun.

The presence of the shell casing in the pistol's chamber could indicate, he said, that someone had grabbed the gun's slide as it was fired, thereby preventing ejection.

Did David Bell grab the gun while it was in the hands of his assailant?

Autopsy reports revealed that the fatal shot had been fired at Bell from no closer than one inch and no further than three feet. So the pistol had been within the victim's reach, and Barbara Bell's attorney contended that David might have caused his own death by grabbing the gun and causing it to fire.

"It could have been his finger on the trigger," the attorney suggested.

Police Corporal Paul Eskridge reported that Barbara Bell had been overwrought and in tears on the night of the tragedy.

"She said she had shot her husband. It was an accident. She said she was unfamiliar with firearms but believed the pistol to be unloaded when she went to the garage to scare him. When he pulled up ... he tried to grab the gun."

"Barbara Bell clearly believed the gun was unloaded," her attorney claimed. "All she had to hang on to was that he didn't lie to her. She went and got a gun to make this non-communicative husband talk to her ... Barbara Bell made a tragic mistake. She is not a criminal."

Officers Kim York and Coonie Evans who had remained with Barbara Bell at police headquarters into the early hours of the morning, awaiting news of the wounded doctor's condition said.

"She kept saying that she didn't do anything wrong — all she did was a point a gun at him to scare him."

At 4 a.m. Officer Evans had asked Mrs. Bell to change her clothes, since the blood-spattered apparel she wore would be needed as evidence.

"She took off her wedding ring and threw it at us," Evans said. "I tried to give it back to her ... She wouldn't take it back."

Barbara Bell told the officers that although her husband said he'd been paged by the hospital, she knew he was lying. She went to a cupboard in the master bedroom and retrieved a gun, the 9mm semi-automatic pistol. She laid the gun on the washing machine as she waited for her husband to return. She became impatient and called him at the hospital, but while he was being paged she heard him approach.

As he came into the garage she met him. She demanded to know where he had been. He said he had been at the hospital.

"No, you weren't," she contradicted him.

"I must have been in the back room," he countered.

"No," she told him. "You weren't."

He then told her that he was out "driving around." She levelled the gun at him.

"I'm going to blow your head off," she told her husband.

David Bell grabbed for the gun.

"She couldn't understand why he did that," Officer York later testified, "since he knew it was loaded."

On January 28th, 1993, Barbara Bell was charged with first-degree murder, which could have carried the death penalty.

"Nobody else pulled that trigger. Barbara Bell pulled that trigger," declared Assistant District Attorney Sam Cook at her two-week trial.

The defence failed to persuade the jury that the shooting was accidental, but Barbara Bell escaped the death penalty. She was convicted of the lesser offence of second-degree murder, and on November 3rd, 1993, Judge Clifford Hopper sentenced her to serve a life term in the Oklahoma State Penitentiary.

No secret bank accounts or million dollar windfalls in the next scenario . . .

17
DEVIL BITCH FROM HELL

Charles Sasser

"I almost expected her head to revolve on her shoulders and green stuff to come out of her mouth"

OKLAHOMA frost still crusted windscreens when the call came in to the Tulsa County Sheriff's Department about 7.40 a.m. on November 20th, 1993.

"There's a guy in a locked car behind our building. Maybe he's just sleeping hard, but I think he's dead," the caller said.

Minutes later Detectives Gary Ross and Matt Palmer pulled their unmarked car into the parking area of Bowen's Carpet Center on Charles Page Boulevard.

Next to the store, partly hidden from the street by a building, sat a blue 1988 Hyundai four-door saloon. A man was slumped on the front passenger seat with his head resting against the window.

A knock on the window failed to arouse him. He appeared to be in his mid-20s and had light brown shoulder-length hair. He looked somewhat lanky, about 6 feet tall. His body was partly covered with a blanket, which reached halfway up his chest, leaving exposed his white pullover with the logo "No Fear" printed across the front. All four doors of the vehicle were locked.

The officers noted a blood smear, powder burns, and possible bullet-holes obscuring the words "No Fear." Detective Ross used a "Slim Jim" tool to get the Hyundai's back door open. That done, he quickly determined that the man inside had been dead perhaps 10 to 12 hours.

Two bullet-holes were in the victim's chest. The powder burns on his shirt made it clear that he had been shot at point-blank range, which would be the distance between two people sitting in the front seat of the car. One of the bullets had passed through the victim and the back of the front seat, dropping onto the floor. The angle of the shot indicated that the victim had been behind the steering-wheel when the bullets struck him.

"All we know is that when we came in to work this morning the car was there with him in it," said one of the employees at the carpet store. "It hadn't been there Saturday. We don't know about Sunday since we were closed."

The detectives recovered two spent .380 cartridge casings ejected from a semi-automatic firearm onto the front floorboard and the seat of the vehicle. Underneath the driver's seat lay a blue-steel Llama .380 semi-automatic pistol.

"Same calibre. Must be the death weapon," a medical investigator surmised. "It looks like a possible suicide."

Detective Ross thought not.

"It's a homicide," he said. "The gun underneath the seat is not the one that killed him. Look, the hammer is cocked. There's no live round in the chamber as there would have been had the gun been recently fired. Somebody else lit up this guy with a different three-eighty."

He also noted two other facts that supported his theory. First there was the position of the driver's seat. Second there was the smear of blood on the seat between the body and the steering-wheel.

"This guy didn't drive himself here," Ross explained.

"He was killed somewhere else and driven here by another person — by a very, very small driver. Probably a woman, but maybe an extremely tiny man. Or even a kid. But I'd bet on a woman."

The victim was a tall man with long legs. Even with his own shorter legs, Ross could not have easily squeezed behind the steering-wheel. The seat had been shifted all the way forward to allow a much smaller person to drive.

The smear of blood on the seat was consistent with the bullet-hole in the back of the seat: the victim had been behind the steering-wheel when he was shot, but had then been moved to the passenger side. The killer had then shifted the seat forward to allow for his or her smaller stature, and had driven the dead or dying man to Charles Page Boulevard. From the looks of it, the killer had carefully, almost tenderly, draped a blanket over the victim before abandoning him.

"It is a gesture a stranger wouldn't ordinarily extend to his victim," Detective Ross observed. "The shooter is probably acquainted — and perhaps well acquainted — with the dead guy."

The contents of the wallet found in the dead man's jeans identified him as 24-year-old Donald James Selige, who turned out to have a long police record of narcotics convictions. He was suspected of being a drug dealer. The wallet contained no money.

Papers found inside the car listed Selige's address as an apartment he shared with his common-law wife, Bernice Land, in Tulsa.

As Detectives Ross and Palmer drove there they wondered aloud: how big a woman was Bernice Land?

She wasn't at home. Her mother said she was out looking for "D.J.," as Donald Selige was commonly called.

"Bernice and D.J. are separated," the woman said. "D.J. has been dating some girl named Nita. Nita called Bernice about six-thirty this morning and asked if she knew where D.J. was. That was real odd. Bernice and Nita don't exactly get along, as you can imagine. This was the first time Nita has ever phoned here."

Bernice's mother did not know Nita's last name, or where she lived. When Bernice Lane herself returned home she too proved to be of little help when it came to Nita, although one look at her figure showed that she at least could not have driven D.J.'s Hyundai to where it was found. She was seven months pregnant.

"We have 'caller ID' on our telephone," Bernice told the detectives. "I don't know Nita's address, but the 'ID' recorded her phone number the first time she called this morning and no one answered."

The number checked out to an address on West 38th Street North. Ross dialled the number and a man answered identifying himself as Tommy Brown.

"I need to talk to Nita," Ross said.

A woman came to the phone.

"Nita, this is Detective Gary Ross of the sheriff's department. I need to talk to you."

A long silence followed. Then the woman said, "I'll meet you at my house." She gave an address not far from where Donald Selige had ended up dead.

Nita lived there with a couple of family members. The detectives arrived ahead of her. One of Nita's sisters, Candy, was, like Bernice Land, pregnant, so it was unlikely that she could have got behind the wheel of the abandoned Hyundai. As they interviewed Candy, Ross and Palmer detected a strong rivalry between her and Nita.

"We found D.J. Selige shot to death this morning," Detective Ross said.

"That bitch!" Candy blurted out.

"Who are you referring to?" Ross asked.

"Nita! That bitch probably killed him!"

The investigators learned that Selige had arrived at the house around eight o'clock the previous evening. While there he jubilantly flashed a bankroll of $7,000, counting the notes to impress the women.

Nita and Selige left the house around 10 p.m. in his

Hyundai after Selige and one of the women did a line of "crank" together. Crank is a powerful synthetic methamphetamine.

"Did Nita have a gun?" one of the detectives asked.

"Yes," Candy answered. Then she seemed to change her mind and went on to say, "Maybe not. Maybe they just had D.J.'s gun. He always carried a blue-steel semi-automatic pistol."

Candy said that Nita returned home at about 5 a.m., apparently in some distress. "I can't believe that S.O.B. did that!" she exclaimed as she walked in. "He left me at the Git 'N Go on Charles Page Boulevard — and I ain't seen the S.O.B. since." Then Nita telephoned a friend, and her demeanour changed suddenly from rage to concern.

"Have you seen D.J.?" she asked, speaking into the receiver. "I'm scared. I'm afraid something has happened to him."

Candy said that Tommy Brown picked up Nita in his car a short time later. Nita said she was going to look for Selige. That had been over nine hours ago.

When she finally walked in she was accompanied by Tommy Brown. The waiting detectives exchanged glances.

With stringy blonde hair, 20-year-old Nita Lynn Carter was only five feet tall. She could have slipped quite comfortably behind the Hyundai's steering-wheel. Moreover, like Selige, she had a police "rap sheet" for narcotics violations.

In her first statement at headquarters she said that Selige had a .380-calibre semi-automatic pistol stuck into his waistband when they left her home around 10 p.m. on Sunday. She did not know if he had money or drugs on him, but she herself did not carry a weapon, nor did she own one.

The couple drove straight to nearby Charles Page Boulevard, where he let her out at the Git 'N Go convenience store. She said he told her that he had to meet "a couple of guys" to transact a "dope deal." Nita said that he was peddling crank.

"That's the last time I see him," she said finally.

The detectives noted her odd demeanour during questioning. She stared blankly, silently, when they asked her questions that she seemed not to want to answer. It was as though she had turned off some light behind her eyes. Between turning herself off and responding to the interrogation, she kept sniffing herself, smelling her arms.

Next the detectives summoned Tommy Brown to the interrogation room. Meanwhile a female secretary escorted Nita to the toilet. The secretary later described Nita's eyes as looking "possessed."

"I almost expected her head to revolve on her shoulders and green stuff to come out of her mouth," the secretary later commented. "She looked like the Devil Bitch from Hell."

The secretary refused to stay in the room with Nita. She left the lavatory and waited in the hallway.

In his first statement Tommy Brown claimed that he knew nothing about what happened to Selige. All he knew was that Nita had shown up at his house that Monday morning, saying that D.J. was missing.

Outside the interrogation room Nita suddenly burst into tears and demanded to speak to the detectives again.

"Tommy had nothing to do with it!" she cried. "I'll tell everything I know." And then once again she started sniffing herself. "I can smell blood!" she explained. "*His* blood."

Hearing this, the detectives thought they were about to get a confession. Instead Nita said she had lied about not having seen D.J. after he dropped her off at the Git 'N Go. She had waited at the store for about 30 minutes, and then walked to the alley where D.J. was supposed to meet his dope customers.

There she found him shot twice in the chest and slumped over his steering-wheel. While she stood there in shock two men in a car entered the alley. Apparently they were the killers, and they had returned to make sure that D.J. was dead. Nita said she dropped to the ground to hide until the men checked out their handiwork and left.

"Describe the men and their car," Ross prompted.

But she couldn't it was dark, she said. Besides, she was lying on the ground in terror, not daring to look up lest the killers saw her.

After they left, Nita said, she pulled D.J.'s body to the passenger's side of his vehicle and got behind the wheel herself. She drove to the carpet centre, where she parked. She said Selige begged her, "Nita, help me!"

She covered him with a blanket and sat with him until he died.

"Why didn't you drive him to a hospital?" Ross asked.

"I — I don't know ... I can smell his blood on me ..."

What she smelled, the investigators suspected, was her conscience. But she could be telling the truth. Drug-abusers often behave irrationally, and a $7,000 roll of cash and a load of crank might well have enticed a pair of killers.

"We'll be talking to you again," Detective Ross told Nita as she left.

Tommy Brown, warned by the police that he could be implicated in a homicide if he lied to protect his lover, soon had a change of heart.

In his revised statement he said that Nita Carter had telephoned him around 11.30 p.m. on Sunday, November 21st, and asked him to pick her up at a bar next door to the Gut 'N Go store.

"I knew she had done something, just not what," he told the investigators. "She had a lot of money and some drugs ... When we got to my house she couldn't take enough showers to get clean. She just kept taking showers."

"Trying to get the smell of blood off," Detective Ross surmised. "I guess it didn't work."

Tommy Brown went on to explain that he had intended to go deer-hunting early on Monday morning with a friend. When the buddy arrived at Brown's home Nita inexplicably stepped to the back door and fired a .380-calibre semi-automatic pistol into the garden.

"This goddamn gun jammed on me last night!" she exclaimed.

While Brown said he could not explain why he did it — it was just something he felt he had to do — he wrapped Nita's .380 in a sock and handed it to his hunting friend.

"Get rid of this," he instructed him.

Detectives Palmer and Ross traced Brown's hunting buddy, who took them to Thieland Lake. There he threw a stone to show where he had hurled the gun into the water. Police divers recovered the weapon, which was found to have fired the bullets which killed Selige.

Meanwhile Ross learned that Nita had paid her lawyer a $1,000 retainer in crisp $100 notes like those D.J. had flashed around on the night he died.

And Candy now came forward to add to her earlier statement. She now said that Nita had a .380 calibre semi-automatic pistol which she had obtained from their mutual boy friend Joe Todd, later practising shooting with it at another friend's home. Detectives recovered bullets fired during that practice. They matched the gun retrieved from the lake. And Todd confirmed that Nita had taken the pistol from his house.

Charged with Selige's murder, Nita Carter continued to profess her innocence right up to her trial in June 1944, when she changed her tune and pleaded guilty.

She is now serving a 25-year-sentence in the Oklahoma State Penitentiary. The police call her conviction and the murder of Donald James "D.J." Selige a "twofer." Her crime took two criminals off the streets — herself and her victim, who was himself an often-convicted crook.

18

RECIPE FOR MURDER

Richard Devon

Told to bring Harold's trousers, sulphur, and red onions

REBECCA SMITH was worried. Her 49-year-old husband, Harold Dean Smith, was away on a fishing trip, but there had been no response to her repeated attempts to phone him at their holiday mobile home on the coast at Cherry Grove, in southern California, where he was staying.

Fearing something was wrong, she called the North Myrtle Beach police, asking them to check on him. Her request was passed to Patrolman Asa Bailey, and on the afternoon of Tuesday, July 18th, 1989, he drove to the trailer park where the Smiths took their holidays.

The blue Chevrolet truck that Bailey had been told to look for was parked in front of a neat mobile home. Bailey knocked on the door but received no answer. He then walked around, peering in through the trailer's narrow windows. From what little he could see, everything appeared to be in order. At the back door he knocked again but still got no response.

After walking around the trailer and seeing nothing out of place, Bailey went back to the front door and knocked again. As he did so, he noticed that the door near the doorknob was scraped and dented. He tried the door. It was unlocked.

Opening it, he called out, then walked into the small living-room. Next to it was a clean, compact kitchen. The place was neatly kept. If someone had battered and pried his way through the front door to get in he had certainly taken care not to mess things up, Bailey thought.

As he walked down the narrow hall he came to a bedroom on his left. Glancing through its doorway, he did a doubletake. There, half on and half off a bloodstained bed, was the body of a man dressed only in underpants. The man seemed to have been lying face down on the bed before he fell or was dragged off and left nearly standing on his head. Bailey could only see the back of his head, under which there was a large bloodstain on the carpet.

After quickly searching the rest of the mobile home and finding no one or anything else out of the ordinary, Bailey returned to his vehicle and radioed for assistance.

It was shortly after 2 p.m. when other officers arrived. Among them was Chief of Detectives Walt Floyd.

Inspecting the scene, they saw that copious amounts of blood marked the bedroom. Large bloodstains blotted the bedclothing and the floor under the victim's head. Blood also spattered the wall and the shade of a bedside lamp. The stains on the wall and lampshade looked to professional eyes like drops shed in the back-swing of a bloody weapon.

When the body was moved and turned over, it became obvious that the cause of death was a horrific beating. The battering had been so fierce that one eye socket had been crushed and the eyeball knocked out of the victim's head.

Apart from the victim, the investigators found no clue to what might have occurred. Although there were pry marks on the front door, there was no evidence of the type of rummaging and ransacking that usually accompanies home robberies.

While the crime scene search was continuing the phone rang. Detective Floyd answered and found himself talking to Rebecca Smith. As gently as he could, he explained that police had found a dead man in the residence, but he had yet to be identified.

Floyd did not explain that it might not be possible to recognise the dead man's face, even if police had a picture of it, since someone had nearly destroyed it.

Later, that afternoon Mrs. Smith arrived from North Carolina, together with other members of his family, one of whom agreed to identify the body.

Rebecca Smith said that her husband had left their home in Laurinburg on Friday after work and joined her sister's family for a long weekend at North Myrtle Beach. The family had returned to Laurinburg on Sunday evening but Floyd decided to stay on until Monday or Tuesday. On Sunday night Rebecca phoned her husband and asked him to bring something she wanted from the beach resort home next day. Later that evening one of her sister's family had also telephoned to say that she had left a silk blouse at the holiday home and wanted it returned.

On Monday morning, Rebecca began trying to contact her husband by phone again but was unable to get him. She knew he should have been in the holiday home when she called, so she phoned the police.

Detective Floyd then took a statement of the events from Rebecca. She wrote:

"I am married to Harold Dean Smith and have been for fourteen years. My family has a trailer at Cherry Grove. Harold came to the beach Friday, where my sister and her family were already there on vacation. He told me if the fish were biting he'd be home Tuesday, if not, he'd be home on Monday.

"I called him between the hours of ten-thirty and eleven forty-five p.m. Sunday night. He said he had met three men from Alexandria, Virginia, or West Virginia, and that they had been shark fishing and were going back Monday. I believe he said one man's name was Jim. Monday I called at eight a.m. to remind him to bring my sister's blouse home. When I didn't get an answer, I began to worry. I called all day today and then I called the police department."

Investigators immediately set out to locate the three men from Virginia. Meanwhile, as the search for clues continued, detectives discovered that someone had used the toilet in the bathroom but had failed to flush it. They took a sample of the urine still in the toilet bowl. It was found to contain cocaine residue.

An autopsy established that the victim had been struck two or three blows, delivered by an object such as a crowbar, a lead pipe or a baseball bat. His skull had been "cracked like an eggshell." There were no defensive wounds on his powerful arms or hands, indicating that Smith had been asleep when he was attacked, or that he had known and trusted his attacker and was taken by surprise.

The anglers from Virginia were located, and were found to be a trio of middle-aged friends on holiday. They were unable to provide any useful information. It was determined that Harold Smith had never taken drugs, so it had been someone else who had neglected to flush the toilet at the crime scene.

Detectives learned that it was not the victim's habit to sleep in the mobile home's bedroom. His usual choice of a resting place was a comfortable couch.

Had he taken home some female companion that Sunday night? That was highly unlikely, said those who knew Smith well. Nevertheless, the possibility was not ruled out.

From Rebecca Smith, detectives learned that her husband probably had as much as $1,000 in cash on him when he left for his fishing trip. He had just received a hefty bonus from his employer, the Owens-Corning glass manufacturers. Also missing was his wristwatch and a horseshoe-shaped ring set with diamonds.

Neither his widow nor his sister-in-law could suggest a suspect.

But when the focus of the investigation shifted from

South Carolina to the victim's home town, detectives had several surprises. They found themselves delving into devil worship, witchcraft, and some highly unusual family relationships.

Initially, these matters were obscured as the investigators heard a litany of praise for the victim. Friends pointed out that Smith always gave his entire pay packet to his wife, who gave him back $50 a week for spending money.

Fishing was a pleasure he had enjoyed with his three step-sons, although this time, he was going fishing alone, Smith had said, because all the boys were employed full-time and could not join him.

The youngest of the step-sons had been only a toddler when Smith married Rebecca. Smith had raised them "as if they were his own flesh and blood", according to those who knew the family.

A colleague of Smith however, said he had heard that everything was not well domestically with the family. As the investigators delved further, the basis of the trouble seemed to have been Rebecca Smith's interest in other men.

The detectives learned that there was not a great deal of life insurance on the victim something over $50,000. There was no indication that Rebecca, who was the beneficiary, had been involved in taking out the policies.

But as the investigators began to look into the possibility that either the widow or the step-sons were involved in Smith's murder, they learned that Rebecca had recently visited a local woman who claimed to be a witch capable of casting spells on people. Rebecca denied any such contact, but the rumours that reached official ears were strongly worded.

Detectives also learned that Rebecca Smith was known to have been consorting with at least two men over several years.

One of Rebecca's supposed lovers was Thad Cason, a workman who when first interviewed denied any knowledge of Smith's murder and could offer no motive for it.

However, when told that detectives knew about his affair with Rebecca Smith and that this made him a suspect, he quickly changed his tune.

Cason said he first met Rebecca some 20 years earlier, long before she married Harold Smith. At that time she was married to the father of her three sons and complained that her husband beat her. It wasn't long after this that Cason and Rebecca began to have an affair, which lasted about two months, Cason said, before she moved out of the state. Over the next 20 years, Cason said, he was married and divorced four times.

Then, some three years before Harold Smith was killed, Cason ran into Rebecca at a store. She was 20 years older but still attractive to him, and memories of that earlier time rekindled his interest.

She didn't put him off, and it wasn't long before they were in bed together again. That affair lasted two years.

Their liaisons were usually in his house, Cason said. On one occasion Rebecca arrived with her son Brian and Brian's girl friend, and while he and Rebecca were in bed together, Brian took photographs of them.

"I couldn't believe it," Cason said. "A mother and her son and the boy's girl friend in bed having sex and taking pictures of each other."

"So you and she had stopped your affair when Harold was killed?" a detective inquired.

"Yeah, I had quit seeing her and she was running around with Billy McGee."

"Who is Billy McGee?"

"He's a thief, and he's Becky's boy friend now."

Cason was asked if the affair had ended on his account or Rebecca's.

"I ended it, because of what she asked me to do."

"And what was that?"

"Well, one afternoon she was at my house on the couch and she asks me if I would do something for her for five thousand dollars. I said, what you want me to do for five thousand dollars, and she said, 'Kill Harold.' I told her I don't get into that, and then she asked me if I knew somebody who would do it. I told her, hell no."

Cason said he knew that Billy McGee had been in prison more than once for theft. He didn't think McGee had the gall to do a killing, but he probably knew somebody from prison who would.

The investigators learned that a young relative of Rebecca's, Charles Gainey, had been living at Cason's house. But he had moved out after Harold Smith was killed and moved in with Rebecca.

In the course of investigating Gainey, detectives learned that the boy had some weird affiliations and was involved in devil worship. He had been working as a dishwasher at the motel which employed Rebecca Smith, who had not returned to work since her husband was murdered.

The motel owner said Rebecca had called in sick several days before the murder, and he had not seen or talked to her since her husband's funeral.

Gainey at first denied any knowledge of Harold Smith's murder. However, the youth was extremely nervous and, as investigators pressed him he unravelled his first version of events on the night the killing took place at Cherry Grove.

Gainey said that on that weekend, Brian Locklear, one of Rebecca's sons from a previous marriage, called at Cason's house and picked him up. When the two got to Rebecca's house, she was there with Billy McGee. Rebecca said they were going to take Brian to the beach so he could go fishing with Harold.

The four of them took the car belonging to another of Rebecca's sons who was working at the time. Brian drove. Gainey said that as they were travelling to the beach they hit some kind of animal.

"I knew something bad was going to happen after that," he said.

"Do you know who killed Harold Smith?"

"It was Billy Ray McGee," he answered.

Gainey told investigators that he wanted them to take

him back to North Myrtle Beach because he feared for his life if he remained in Laurinburg. He said McGee had warned him not to talk to the police about the events at Cherry Grove. In subsequent statements, however, he said it was Rebecca Smith who had killed her husband and who had warned him not to talk to the police about it.

Continuing with his story, Gainey said that when they arrived at the beach, they stopped at a fishing pier for a short time and then drove to the mobile-home park. Rebecca had told Brian to leave the lights off when he drove up and not to park in front of Harold's trailer.

"She told me and Billy to lie down in the back seat so Harold wouldn't know she had a car load of people with her," Gainey said.

With Gainey and Billy hidden in the back seat, Brian and Rebecca went inside the trailer's screened porch and knocked on the front door. A light came on, and Harold came to the door to let them in. At that time, Gainey said, he didn't understand why Rebecca was holding a baseball bat.

Rebecca and Brian had been inside the house for a few minutes when Brian came back out to the car and said Rebecca wanted them to go back to the pier and get a soft drink. Gainey said they were gone about 10 minutes. When they returned, Rebecca came out of the house saying, "I did it, I did it. He's dead."

All three of them then entered the trailer. Gainey was ordered to go down the hall and "look at what Becky had done." Harold was making gurgling noises, so Brian took the baseball bat and hit his stepfather with it again "to finish him off."

Gainey then described how Brian Locklear had used lotion to remove the horseshoe ring from his stepfather's finger, and Rebecca went around the house wiping things down so there would be no fingerprints.

As they were leaving, the witness said, Billy McGee smashed the door with the baseball bat, saying that would lead police to think there had been a break-in.

Upon returning to Laurinburg, Rebecca told Gainey and Brian to take the horseshoe ring to the root doctor, as payment for her previous efforts to kill Harold by witchcraft. Gainey said that on the root doctor's instructions, he and Brian returned home to fetch a pair of Harold's trousers. They put these into a cake pan along with some sulphur and red onions, and then burned the whole mess. This, Gainey told investigators, was the root doctor's "medicine to keep the police off Rebecca's trail."

Investigators paid a visit to the root doctor, who denied knowing anything about the diamond horseshoe ring or any efforts to put a death spell on Harold Smith.

On August 8th, 1989, Rebecca Smith and Billy Ray McGee were arrested and charged with the murder of Harold Dean Smith. Gainey and Brian Locklear were charged as accessories.

With information provided by Gainey, officers found a baseball bat that had been tossed off a bridge over the Waccamaw River. It was bloodstained and bore paint that matched paint on the door at the murder scene.

Shortly after her arrest, Rebecca Smith gave police a statement in which she laid the blame for the murder on Billy McGee. She admitted making the trip to Cherry Grove but said it was McGee who had struck her husband with the baseball bat.

Brian Locklear also told investigators that it was McGee who had murdered his stepfather, but McGee denied the slaying. However, when he learned that the other members of the quartet had implicated him, he came up with his own version.

He said that he had met Rebecca some time before his last jail stay, and they began having an affair.

Then, when he was returned to prison two years before Harold Smith was killed, Rebecca began coming to visit him, each time bringing him spending money. Prior to this, she had given him cash to buy cocaine.

During her prison visits Rebecca had talked about getting rid of Harold so she could be with McGee when he got out. She told him she had been going to a root doctor to put a spell on Harold.

This was either to make her husband sick or to kill him. After his release, McGee said, he went with Rebecca at least 20 times to see the root doctor.

On the night of the murder, he continued, he and Rebecca had smoked a joint and snorted cocaine before heading out to the beach.

McGee insisted that he never went into the bedroom where Harold Smith was, but he said that at one point, he heard Harold calling for Rebecca to help him. He claimed that Locklear later handed him the baseball bat to be tossed into the river.

In December 1990, Rebecca Smith went on trial for her life. She admitted she was an accessory in her husband's murder, having been present when McGee beat Harold Smith to death with the baseball bat, but she denied having anything else to do with the killing.

Brian Locklear continued to maintain that Billy McGee had done the deed, but when McGee's turn on the stand came, he recalled that Locklear, on the way back to Laurinburg after the murder, said to him, "Billy, you can be my daddy now.

Rebecca Smith was convicted and sentenced to death, but a retrial was ordered after it was maintained that allowing evidence about her cocaine use had been prejudicial.

In the meantime, Billy McGee and Brian Locklear had begun serving 35-year sentences for their part in the crime. Charles Gainey, who was sentenced to 15 years, was already out on parole.

At Rebecca Smith's retrial in February 1994, Brian Locklear took the stand to say it was he who had beaten his stepfather to death with the baseball bat and that his mother had nothing to do with it.

Under cross-examination, he admitted he was bisexual and had been tested HIV-positive.

"You have nothing to lose do you?" the prosecutor

asked the man whose disease was a virtual death sentence.

Again, the jury found Rebecca Smith guilty of first-degree murder, but they declined to give her the death penalty. She was sentenced to life imprisonment.